NEW MERM KU-538-433

General editor: Brian Gibbons
Professor of English Literature, University of Münster

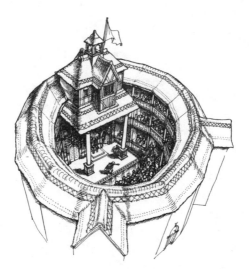

Reconstruction of an Elizabethan theatre
by C.Walter Hodges

NEW MERMAIDS

Christopher
Marlowe

The Jew
of Malta

edited by James R. Siemon

Boston University

A & C Black • London
W W Norton • New York

FOR
RUTH A. SIEMON
AND
RALPH M. SIEMON

Second edition 1994
Reprinted 1997, 1999
A & C Black (Publishers) Limited
35 Bedford Row, London WC1R 4JH
ISBN 0–7136–3792–7

First published in this form 1966
Ernest Benn Limited

Published in the United States of America
by W.W. Norton & Company, Inc.
500 Fifth Avenue, New York, NY 10110
ISBN 0–393–90070–3

CIP catalogue records for this book
are available from the British Library
and the Library of Congress.

Filmset in Plantin by
Selwood Systems, Midsomer Norton
Printed and bound in Great Britain by
Biddles of Guildford Limited

CONTENTS

ACKNOWLEDGEMENTS

It is a pleasure to acknowledge the help and encouragement of colleagues, friends and students. From early to late, Professor Brian Gibbons offered suggestions and enthusiastic support. Professor David Bevington shared his knowledge and insight at a particularly important time in the evolution of the project. Professor Emily Bartels read over the introduction and generously allowed me to read her work in progress. And, with characteristic generosity, Professor William Carroll provided help and prevented more than a few errors. Students in my classes in Renaissance drama at Boston University provided a never-failing stimulus to further thinking about *The Jew of Malta* and, particularly, to consideration of the issues it raises for our own day.

JAMES R. SIEMON

ABBREVIATIONS

I have followed standard practice in referring to the first quarto edition of *The Jew of Malta* (1633) as Q. Other abbreviations are as follows:

Editions

Bawcutt	N. W. Bawcutt, ed., *The Jew of Malta* (Revels Plays), London, 1978
Bennett	H. S. Bennett, ed., *The Jew of Malta and The Massacre at Paris*, London, 1931
Bowers	Fredson Bowers, ed., *The Complete Works of Christopher Marlowe*, Cambridge, 1981
Craik	T. W. Craik, ed., *The Jew of Malta* (New Mermaids), London, 3rd impression, 1979
Steane	J. B. Steane, ed., *The Complete Plays of Christopher Marlowe*, Harmondsworth, 1969
Van Fossen	Richard W. Van Fossen, ed., *The Jew of Malta* (Regents), Lincoln, Neb., 1964

Periodicals

CE	*Cahiers Elisabéthains*
ELH	*English Literary History*
ELR	*English Literary Renaissance*
JEGP	*Journal of English and Germanic Philology*
JWCI	*Journal of the Warburg and Courtauld Institutes*
MLQ	*Modern Language Quarterly*
RenD	*Renaissance Drama*
RES	*Review of English Studies*
RORD	*Research Opportunities in Renaissance Drama*
SQ	*Shakespeare Quarterly*
ShakS	*Shakespeare Studies*
TJHSE	*Transactions of the Jewish Historical Society of England*
TLS	*The Times Literary Supplement*

Miscellaneous

Gentillet	Innocent Gentillet, *A Discourse Upon the Meanes of Well Governing ... A Kingdom* (trans. Simon Patericke, London, 1602)
Hunter	G. K. Hunter, 'The Theology of Marlowe's *The Jew of Malta*', *JWCI* 27 (1964), 211–40

Tilley   M. P. Tilley, *A Dictionary of the Proverbs in England
                    in the Sixteenth and Seventeenth Centuries,* Ann
                    Arbor, Mich., 1950

Biblical quotations are from *The Geneva Bible: A Facsimile of the
1560 Edition* (Madison, Wis., 1969). Shakespeare is quoted from
David Bevington, ed., *The Complete Works of Shakespeare* (4th
edition, New York, 1992). Quotations from Kyd's *Spanish
Tragedy* are from the New Mermaid edition of J. R. Mulryne
(1989); quotations from *Dr Faustus* are from the New Mermaid
edition of Roma Gill (1989); otherwise, Marlowe quotations are
from the edition of J. B. Steane (1969).

INTRODUCTION

THE AUTHOR

IN 1564 CHRISTOPHER MARLOWE was born in Canterbury to the
family of a shoe-maker, John Marlowe, who had his own shop
and would eventually hold several positions of professional and
civic authority, but who also was repeatedly sued for non-
payment of debts and rent.[1] Marlowe entered King's School,
Canterbury, probably as a charity student, in 1578. In 1580 he
enrolled at Corpus Christi College, Cambridge, where, as the
holder of an Archbishop Matthew Parker scholarship, he received
the B.A. in 1584. Thereafter, his attendance became sporadic,
with frequent lengthy absences. These evidently led to rumours
that he had fled to Rheims to study at the Catholic seminary, for
his reputation was defended against such rumours when the
Privy Council intervened to order the granting of his M.A. in
1587, insisting, somewhat cryptically, that he had done 'good
service . . . touching the benefit of his country'. Thus, as early as
1587 there is reason to believe that Marlowe was involved in
intrigue at the very highest official level. But he was also, while
still at Cambridge, apparently writing some of the literary and
dramatic works that have survived to us. Although the dating is
imprecise, there is general agreement that Marlowe's translations
of Ovid's *Amores* and Lucan's *Civil Wars* along with his drama
Dido Queen of Carthage, which is based on Book VI of Virgil's
Aeneid, were probably written in the years that preceded his
move to London and the enormous success of *Tamburlaine I* and
II in 1587–8.

Between 1587, when he left for London, and his murder in a
Deptford tavern on 30 May 1593, Marlowe wrote four more
plays and the epyllion *Hero and Leander*, saw published the only
one of his works printed during his life (*Tamburlaine* in 1590),
was arrested five times and accumulated quite a reputation. After
the enormous documentable public responses to *Tamburlaine*,
the evidence is less certain about the order of the other works.
We do know that he and the playwright Thomas Kyd shared a
room in 1591, and that by the beginning of 1592 *The Jew of
Malta*, which frequently echoes Kyd's *Spanish Tragedy*, was being

[1] Among biographies of Marlowe, the most extensive treatment of his early years is
provided by William Urry, *Christopher Marlowe and Canterbury* (London, 1988). Also
useful are Mark Eccles, *Christopher Marlowe in London* (Cambridge, Mass., 1934) and
F.S. Boas, *Christopher Marlowe: A Biographical and Critical Study* (Oxford, 1940).

performed, while no record authenticates a performance of *Edward II* before the end of 1592 or of *Doctor Faustus* before Marlowe's death. It would not be unreasonable to suggest that *The Jew of Malta* (1591?) follows *Tamburlaine* (1587) in composition and precedes the other two plays. For reasons of thematic similarity, *The Massacre at Paris* is often assumed to be roughly the contemporary of *The Jew of Malta*.

Marlowe's arrests are more precisely dated, but their implications are not clear-cut. He was arrested in 1589 for being present at the killing of William Bradley by the poet Thomas Watson, but he was not imprisoned for very long. Three times in 1592 he was subjected to arrest: in January in Flushing, apparently a centre of espionage activities, for counterfeiting; in May in London for threats against the constable and beadle of the Holywell area; and in September in Canterbury for assault. None of these occasions is without complicating factors, nor did any of them result in substantial penalty. However, in May of 1593 the Privy Council ordered Marlowe's arrest, with instructions to seek him at the house of Sir Thomas Walsingham. The basis for this arrest is not certain, but detailed accusations by Thomas Kyd (himself undergoing investigation and torture) and later by the informer Richard Baines charging Marlowe with blasphemy and promoting atheism have survived from this period.[2] On 20 May he appeared before the Star Chamber and was ordered to report daily thereafter. On 30 May he was killed in a Deptford tavern, where he had gone to meet with three men, two of whom had frequently been involved in clandestine activities. The coroner's jury excused the killer, Ingram Friser, with a ruling of self-defence.

By the time of his death at the age of twenty-nine, Christopher Marlowe had a well-established reputation. Despite the popularity of his plays and despite acclaim from writers like Peele, who termed him the 'Muses darling', appreciations of his intelligence and skill, like those of *The Second Part of the Return from Parnassus*, are mixed with moral disapproval for the man himself:

> Marlowe was happy in his buskined muse,
> Alas unhappy in his life and end.
> Pitty it is that wit so ill should dwell,
> Wit lent from heaven, but vices sent from hell.[3]

[2] For the Baines charges, see Paul H. Kocher, *Christopher Marlowe: A Study of His Thought, Learning, and Character* (New York, 1946), pp. 33–68. On the Flushing episode, see R.B. Wernham, 'Christopher Marlowe at Flushing in 1592', *English Historical Review* 91 (1976), 344–5.

[3] Cited from Millar Maclure, ed., *Marlowe: The Critical Heritage 1588–1896* (London, 1979), p. 46. For recent views, see John Russell Brown, ed., *Marlowe: 'Tamburlaine*

Those contemporaries who claimed to know him or to know of him typically employed negative terms – atheism, disrespect for authority, cruelty, violence, Machiavellianism – in their descriptions. Yet in those very terms of disapproval for the man, there may be suggestions of that combination of qualities – cosmic irony, sardonic humour, intellectual aspiration, powerful spectacle, impassioned verse and detached analysis – that have won his works four hundred years of increasingly positive response.

DATE AND SOURCES

With its initial allusions to the death of the Duke of Guise (assassinated in December 1588) as 'now', the Prologue to Marlowe's *Jew of Malta* has suggested to most scholars a date of composition some time from 1589 to 1591. The play is first referred to in Philip Henslowe's diary, which records some thirty-six performances between 26 February 1592 and 21 June 1596, allowing for an interim from July 1592 to December 1593 during which the London theatres were closed by order of the Privy Council owing to the danger of plague. Its initial popularity was apparently substantial, with ten recorded (and profitable) performances between February and June 1592, a revival in the one month of playing allowed during the plague closing and subsequent performances in 1594, 1596 and evidently in 1601, when Henslowe's diary records purchases of 'divers thinges for the Jewe of malta'.[4]

The earliest surviving edition of the play dates from 1633, and that quarto edition, once thought to be the product of an adapter but now generally accepted as the work of Marlowe, records the revival of the play by Queen Henrietta's company, who played both at court and at the Cockpit or Phoenix theatre. Thomas Heywood's prologues to this edition supply the information that the famous Elizabethan actor Edward Alleyn had originally played the part of Barabas. No further performances are recorded in England (though apparently some version of the play, entitled *Tragödie von Barabas, Juden von Malta*, was enacted in Germany during the seventeenth century) until a single nineteenth-century

---

the Great', 'Edward II', and 'The Jew of Malta': A Casebook (London, 1982); Harold Bloom, ed., *Christopher Marlowe: Modern Critical Views* (New York, 1986). Annotated bibliographies of recent Marlowe criticism are: Jonathan F.S. Post, 'Recent Studies in Marlowe (1968–1976)', *ELR* 7 (1977), 382–99; Ronald Levao, 'Recent Studies in Marlowe (1977–1986)', *ELR* 18 (1988), 329–42.

[4] See R.A. Foakes and R.T. Rickert, eds., *Henslowe's Diary* (Cambridge, 1961), p. 170.

revival of the play in adapted form took place in 1818.[5] Aspects of this revival and of some twentieth-century productions are discussed below.

There is no known general source for Marlowe's play. However, as is always the case with the works of Marlowe, *The Jew of Malta* makes pointed use of copious allusions and participates in complex dialogues with contemporary issues and discourses. Sixteenth-century history contributes the famous 1565 Turkish siege of Christian Malta that forms the international setting for Barabas's tragedy and, along with the fact of the siege, contributes as well potentially interesting ambiguities of significance. The repulsed siege of Malta was not only known as a Christian victory over Islam, but it was also the subject of contemporary rumours about financial complicity between the Jews and the Turks, who were said to have joined forces because the aggressive raids of Malta's Knights had turned it into an infamous market for enslaved captives.[6] Some have also suggested general relationships between the story of Barabas and that of the famous Joseph Nasi, a Jew who, with the backing of the Turks, became Duke of the Island of Naxos and engaged in other conflict with Christian forces in the Mediterranean.[7]

There may have been no professing Jews in Marlowe's England, since they had been banished in 1290 and would not in theory be readmitted, except as converts to Christianity, until 1656, but *The Jew of Malta* obviously draws upon a widely shared European tradition and discourse of anti-Semitism.[8] Even if the inherited English prejudice, unlike its Continental varieties, had no genuine object upon which to vent itself, the English stage frequently made reference to Jews and Judaism and the sixteenth century saw periodic episodes of violence against suspected Jews. One of these episodes, in fact – the persecution of Queen Elizabeth's Jewish physician, Dr Roderigo Lopez, in 1594 – may have

[5] E.K. Chambers, *The Elizabethan Stage* (Oxford, 1923), vol. 3, p. 425

[6] On the siege, see Brian Blouet, *The Story of Malta* (London, 1967); for rumours that Suleiman financed the siege with loans from Jewish bankers, see p. 53; cf. Cecil Roth, 'The Jews of Malta', *TJHSE* 12 (1928–31), 187–251 (p. 216).

[7] On references to Nasi, alias Joao or Juan Miguez, in sixteenth-century sources, see Ethel Seaton, 'Fresh Sources for Marlowe', *RES* 5 (1929), 390–3; Cecil Roth, *The House of Nasi: The Duke of Naxos* (Philadelphia, 1948).

[8] Even in the absence of professing Jews, the category of 'Jew' in sixteenth-century England is a highly complex construct, with political, theological, economic and moral dimensions. Professing Jews were banished from England from the reign of Edward I (1290) to Cromwell's Protectorate (1656), but there were groups of so-called 'new Christians' or Marranos – outward converts to Christianity, usually of Portuguese origin – in England throughout the intervening period. On the Jewish communities of the Elizabethan period, some of which appear to have been secretly practising their

had something to do with the later popularity of *The Jew of Malta* and that of Shakespeare's *Merchant of Venice* (1594–8?).[9] While few other dramas of the period treat Jewish protagonists as extensively as these two, the language of the stage – like that of Elizabethan culture generally – routinely alludes to Jews and Jewishness as compounded of diabolical opposition to Christianity, cruelty (to the extent of ritual cannibalism and mass-poisoning), treachery, usury, avarice, legalism, sharp practice, tribalism and physical repulsiveness.[10] Marlowe's play obviously deploys virtually every element of this anti-Semitic inheritance in constructing Barabas – but the question of the ends to which it is put will demand further discussion.

The play's other sorts of allusions have sources many and varied. Its use of proverbs, like its practice of classical allusion, is always loaded with implication; for compact illustration, see the end of the first scene with its proverbial wisdom about violence (I.i.131; cf. Tilley, N 321) and self-interest (I.i.185; cf. Tilley, N 57), its references to Iphigenia (I.i.137) and its quotations from Ovid (I.i.106–10) and, in Latin, from Terence (I.i.188). Biblical allusion is similarly everywhere, its uses and abuses contributing particularly powerful ironies – as, for example, in Barabas's dismissive treatment of Job's trials as a lesser version of his own (I.ii.182–99) or in the echoes of the

religion, see Lucien Wolf, 'Jews in Elizabethan England', *TJHSE* 11 (1924–7), 1–91; Cecil Roth, 'The Middle Period of Anglo-Jewish History (1290–1655) Reconsidered', *TJHSE* 19 (1955–9), 1–12, and his *History of the Jews in England* (Oxford, 1964); also Harold Pollins, *Economic History of the Jews in England* (East Brunswick, N.J., 1982). For evidence of positive attitudes towards Judaism during the period, see Theodore K. Rabb, 'The Stirrings of the 1590s and the Return of the Jews to England', *TJHSE* 26 (1974–8), 26–33; also David S. Katz, *Philo-Semitism and the Readmission of the Jews to England 1603–1655* (Oxford, 1982).

[9] On Lopez, see John Gwyer, 'The Case of Dr Lopez', *TJHSE* 16 (1945–51), 163–84. For staging of the two plays during the Lopez period, see Roslyn Knutson, 'Influence of the Repertory System on the Revival and Revision of *The Spanish Tragedy* and *Dr Faustus*', *ELR* 18 (1988), 257–74. For critical assessment of the plays in relation to one another, see Maurice Charney, 'Jessica's Turquoise Ring and Abigail's Poisoned Porridge: Shakespeare and Marlowe as Rivals and Imitators', *RenD* 10 (1979), 33–44; Thomas Cartelli, 'Shakespeare's *Merchant*, Marlowe's *Jew*: The Problem of Cultural Difference', *ShakS* 20 (1988), 255–60; James Shapiro, 'Which is *The Merchant* Here, and Which *The Jew*?', *ShakS* 20 (1988), 269–82.

[10] Stephen Gosson mentions a lost Elizabethan play, *The Jew*, as illustrating 'the greediness of worldly chusers and bloody minds of usurers' (*The School of Abuse* (1579), p. 42 (cited in Chambers, *Elizabethan Stage*, vol. 4, p. 204)). For such charges generally, see Esther L. Panitz, *The Alien in Their Midst: Images of Jews in English Literature* (London, 1981); J.L. Cardozo, *The Contemporary Jew in Elizabethan Drama* (Amsterdam, 1925). Compare the more positive representation of the Jew Gerontus in R. W[ilson]., *The Three Ladies of London* (1584).

story of Christ's passion in Barabas's confrontation with official Malta (I.ii.97–125).[11] The play also makes frequent use of lines, gestures and other formal elements derived from older dramatic forms (such as the moralities), from contemporary drama (particularly Thomas Kyd's *Spanish Tragedy*) and from Marlowe's own works (cf. the parodic use of Marlovian lines by Ithamore).[12] The most obvious contemporary allusion, of course, is the Prologue's famous and much-debated invocation of the spirit of Niccolò Machiavelli.

Scholars have long had difficulty reconciling the pronouncements of Marlowe's 'Machevill' and, more generally, the action of the play as a whole with the actual writings of Machiavelli. The difficulties are chiefly two: Machiavelli treats religion as a vital element of statecraft, while Machevill dismisses it as a 'childish toy'; Machiavelli has nothing to say about economics, while Machevill offers the tragedy of a character whose fortune is said to have been made by his 'means'.[13] Such distortions of Machiavelli's views and interests have often been explained as evidence that Marlowe's play dramatizes the false view derived from the popular anti-Machiavellian polemic that followed Innocent Gentillet's widely known *Anti-Machiavel* (1576) in typifying Machiavellianism as material greed and atheism. More recently, compelling arguments have been made for considering the Prologue and the play as exposing the false Machiavellianism of the polemical tradition to searching irony, presenting the seemingly pious Ferneze as a more satisfactory embodiment of true Machiavellian 'policy', or showing that the Machevill of the polemical tradition is a straw man, and thereby presenting an analysis of ideology as false consciousness.[14]

[11] Judith Weil charts strategic allusions in Marlowe generally (*Christopher Marlowe: Merlin's Prophet* (Cambridge, 1977)); cf. James H. Sims, *Dramatic Uses of Biblical Allusions in Marlowe and Shakespeare* (Gainesville, 1966).

[12] David Bevington describes the indebtedness of Marlowe's art to morality play structure (*From Mankind to Marlowe: Growth of Structure in the Popular Drama of Tudor England* (Cambridge, Mass., 1962), esp. pp. 218–33).

[13] For the political usefulness of religious authority, see, e.g., *The Prince* XI; for Machiavelli's self-proclaimed lack of knowledge 'either about profits or about losses' and hence his fitness only 'to reason about the state', see the letter of 9 April 1513 (cited in Albert O. Hirschman, *The Passions and the Interests: Political Arguments for Capitalism before Its Triumph* (Princeton, 1977), p. 41).

[14] N.W. Bawcutt argues that Marlowe shared his contemporaries' mixed acquaintance with Machiavellianism, deriving a sense of its doctrines from reading of Machiavelli but other ideas from the widespread literature that provided an account of Machiavellianism in order to refute it ('Machiavelli and Marlowe's *The Jew of Malta*', *RenD* 3 (1970), 3–49); compare the account of Catherine Minshull ('Marlowe's "Sound Machevill"', *RenD* 13 (1982), 35–53), who finds Marlowe's play structured by a contrast between the actual theories of Machiavelli (embodied in Ferneze) and the

There should also be added the play's engagement with the heteroglot socio-economic discourses of Elizabethan London. The frequent volatile struggles involving London's population of 'strangers', struggles that had led to an atmosphere of crisis by the early 1590s, inform the language and action of the play. Its treatment of the merchant stranger Barabas as well as its depiction of Maltese anti-Semitism may be seen in an Elizabethan English context, of the anti-foreigner sentiments that produced Parliamentary debate, public insurrection and such dramatic works as the officially censored *Sir Thomas More* (1590–3?), with its depiction of English violence against the specific foreign population in London.[15]

The complexity of *The Jew of Malta*'s ironies, the multiplicity of issues it treats and the numerous discourses it employs have perhaps contributed to the frequently reiterated modern charge that the play lacks unity.[16] But theatrical discontinuity, as Brecht has maintained, may have its own logic and value, and the power of Renaissance drama to disturb ideological complacency may be felt most strongly in its discontinuities.[17] *The Jew of Malta* is

popular distortion of them in Gentillet's account of Machiavellians as greedy and loving evil for its own sake; cf. Bob Hodge ('Marlowe, Marx, and Machiavelli: Reading into the Past' in David Aers et al., eds., *Literature, Language and Society in England 1580–1680* (Dublin, 1981), pp. 1–22), who sees the logic of the play's plot contradicting that of the Prologue and suggesting a sense of ideology as false consciousness in Barabas's confusions. Thomas Cartelli argues that Barabas conveniently adopts Machiavellian discourse and its 'spirit of moral abandon' rather than true Machiavellian principles (*Marlowe, Shakespeare and the Economy of Theatrical Experience* (Philadelphia, 1991)).

[15] On the anti-foreigner violence of the early 1590s, see Ian W. Archer, *The Pursuit of Stability: Social Relations in Elizabethan London* (Cambridge, 1991), esp. pp. 131–48; Andrew Pettegree, *Foreign Protestant Communities in Sixteenth-Century London* (Oxford, 1986). Scott McMillin gives a useful account of the situation in relation to the censorship of *Sir Thomas More* in *The Elizabethan Theatre and The Book of Sir Thomas More* (Ithaca, 1987). See also the appendix below, pp. 115–18.

[16] Though now largely rejected as a result of studies of the play's textual features (see Van Fossen, p. xxvii), the opinion was once widely held. In 1910 C.F. Tucker Brooke declared 'All critics of the play have noticed with regret the failure of the last half of *The Jew of Malta* to fulfil the splendid promise of the first two acts. It is beyond question that the vigorous flow of tragic interest and character portrayal with which the play opens wastes away amid what ... is a wilderness of melodrama and farce' (*The Works of Christopher Marlowe* (Oxford, 1910), p. 232). Compare F. P. Wilson, 'To suppose that the same man who wrote the first two acts was wholly responsible for the last three is revolting to sense and sensibility' (*Marlowe and the Early Shakespeare* (Oxford, 1953), p. 65).

[17] For accounts of Elizabethan drama along these lines, see Michael Hattaway, *Elizabethan Popular Theatre: Plays in Performance* (London, 1982); Simon Shepherd, *Marlowe and the Politics of Elizabethan Theatre* (Brighton, 1986), which locates the politics of the Elizabethan theatre in 'the relationship between dominant ideologies

not an easy play to love; it is far easier to hate – or, more typically, to dismiss – but it was probably the most popular play of the Elizabethan era. It represents versions of attitudes and tensions that remain identifiable in the multi-cultural world we inhabit four hundred years later, suggesting reason enough to consider its possible value for our own time, despite its relative neglect by both critic and theatre.

STAGING

The stage history of *The Jew of Malta* before the twentieth century is sparse in detail and instance. From the earliest sixteenth-century performances (1592–8) by various companies and mostly at the Rose, we have the names of the principal actor (Edward Alleyn), evidence of frequent production, references to two physical circumstances (the cauldron in which Barabas dies and his 'artificiall . . . nose') and the probability of a third (a red wig and beard like that later worn by Burbage in the role of Shakespeare's Shylock).[18] The evidence from the seventeenth century records one certain production – that by Queen Henrietta's company at the Cockpit or Phoenix and at court (the source of the single early text of the play from 1633) – and suggests other undocumented performances, perhaps even in excerpted form.[19] While there appear to have been German productions during the seventeenth century, there are no records of further English performance before that of Edmund Kean on 24 April 1818 in an adaptation 'founded on Marlowe's tragedy' but changed to render Barabas an acceptably tragic victim of and revenger upon a corrupt society.[20] This first modern production substituted a prologue by Samuel Penley abjuring anti-Semitic prejudice and stressing moral import and added a scene detailing the love of Lodowick and Mathias for Abigail; cuts removed such objectionable, potentially farcical features as the poisoning of the nuns, the on-stage strangling of Bernardine, the poisoned flowers and the fatal cauldron, while Kean ingeniously interpreted Barabas's catalogue of earlier atrocities as a rhetorical test of Ithamore's allegiance. The early scene of Barabas's victimization and

---

and the questioning/affirming strategies of the individual text' (pp. xvii–xviii); and James R. Siemon, *Shakespearean Iconoclasm* (Berkeley, 1985).

[18] See Hattaway, *Elizabethan Popular Theatre*, p. 81.

[19] See Bawcutt's edition, p. 3.

[20] Most of the information which follows is based on James L. Smith's '*The Jew of Malta* in the Theatre', in Brian Morris, ed., *Christopher Marlowe* (London, 1968), pp. 3–23.

the final scene of his downfall were acclaimed for their 'tragic solemnity' (Smith, p. 9).

The evidence suggests no twentieth-century theatrical successors to this approach, although the aspects of the play with which it struggles are worth keeping in mind. The dominant note of twentieth-century productions has been exactly that farce which Kean's high romantic portrayal attempted to avoid. The first twentieth-century performance was apparently the 1907 Williams College production in Massachusetts, while the first British production was the 1922 Phoenix Society performances at Daly's Theatre in London (Smith, p. 4). Accounts of the 1922 production suggest that it was played as 'a monstrous farce, a careless burlesque of human speech and human action' that emphasized the 'brutality' of Barabas and prompted audience laughter at the deaths of the lovers and the poisoning of the nuns (Smith, p. 11). Later productions would do more to mix tonalities, but the emphasis on farce remains understandably relevant, even when recognition is granted to the play's satiric elements.

The most prominent element of satire in modern productions is already registered in the programme notes to the Reading University production of 1954, which recognized the play's transformation of Barabas from 'suffering and oppressed human figure into . . . "a prodigious caricature" ' and drew attention to the significance of his failures to live up to the demands of Machiavellian strategy as defined by *The Prince*, reasoning that 'the play therefore presents the spectator with the satirically posed problem: Who then are the real villains of the story, the true followers of Machiavelli?' (Smith, p. 13). While the speaker for Machevill's Prologue in this production is significantly listed as '?', the identification of Ferneze as the truer Machiavellian becomes a recurrent feature of subsequent productions. So, in the 1975 Marlowe Society production in Cambridge, directed by John Chapman, Machevill stood at Ferneze's elbow; in the 1985 American Shakespeare Company production directed by Douglas Overtoom at Theatre 22, the parts were doubled; and, most spectacularly, in the 1987 Barry Kyle production at the Swan Theatre in Stratford-upon-Avon (and later at the Barbican), the play closed with Ferneze removing his wig to reveal himself as the Machevill of the Prologue, whose Italian accent was reassumed in the final pious phrases.[21]

While such identification of a satiric object remains a feature of many modern productions, there is widespread recognition

[21] References, respectively, from *RORD* 18 (1975), 61; *RORD* 28 (1985), 165; and *TLS* (31 July 1987), p. 820

that the play's comic energies are broader in deployment than such a narrowly defined target would allow one to conceive of them. Especially revealing in this regard are the major 1964 productions of Peter Cheeseman (Victoria Theatre, Stoke-on-Trent) and Clifford Williams (Aldwych Theatre; recast in Stratford 1965).

Both these interpretations drew upon the model provided by such contemporary dramatic analogues as Joe Orton's *Loot* to conceive *The Jew of Malta* as an instance of what Cheeseman defines as 'the humour of the sick joke, and the black comedy' (Smith, p. 14). In keeping with such conceptions, speedy conjunctions and slapstick physicality were used by Williams to emphasize the play's combinations of contradictory elements and emotions – Barabas spits into the fatal porridge, Bernardine drops the body of the penitent Abigail 'with a bump', Barabas and Ithamore shake hands behind Jacomo's back after framing him for murder, Barabas performs as a Flamenco dancer while the deadly flowers circulate (Smith, pp. 15–18). The audience, released from ordinary moral constraint by entering into the familiar generic expectations of the sick joke, was, according to Cheeseman, prompted to sympathize with Barabas as 'a cynical self-serving businessman' who turns into a 'half-crazy gangster' when abused by 'a crew of grasping Christian hypocrites' (Smith, pp. 19–20). But even this definition does not do justice to the misanthropic generality of Cheeseman's production: in a trebling of roles, the part of Machevill was acted by the same actor (the dramatist Alan Ayckbourn) who played, not Ferneze, but the Spaniard Del Bosco and, most significantly, also one of the Jews (Smith, p. 5). Similarly broad in its indictment of humanity, the self-designated 'gangster epic' (Smith, p. 20) presented by Williams rendered Barabas as a seductively professional wrong-doer among amateurs – what one reviewer called a 'clear sighted opportunist within a society that would act in the same way if it dared'.[22] To this end, Barabas was given a suave, well-groomed, confident demeanour, richly attired and with a silver-tipped forelock, while opposing characters like Ferneze were represented as weakened or diminished. Ferneze might end the play brandishing aloft a cross-shaped sword hilt, but the Williams production deprived him of some of his most aggressive lines (III.v.29–33; V.i.1–2), subordinated him to both Del Bosco and Katherine (in II.ii and III.ii) and actually had him cringe and back away from the Jew (V.v.20). Here farce served the intentions of satire, but that satire was hardly limited to Ferneze's Chris-

[22] *The Times*, 2 October 1965

tianity as its object; rather it aimed instead at what Williams's programme calls 'dollar civilization' (Smith, p. 21).

In keeping with such notions of the breadth of the play's attacks and in response to the fluidity of its own spatiality (e.g. in the frequent mid-scene location changes – I.ii from senate-house to outside; II.iii from slave market to the door of Barabas's house; V.i from inside to outside Malta), costume and settings for modern productions have tended to the abstract. At its simplest, this has resulted in modern-dress performances that add twentieth-century references, such as the 1984 Peter Benedict version that ended with Barabas in a microwave or the 1985 American Shakespeare Company production that started with Barabas totalling his figures on a pocket calculator and ended with his death in an electric chair wired to a time bomb intended to destroy everyone.[23] In staging, there has been performance in the round against a permanent setting, as in the 1964 Stoke-on-Trent production (Smith, p. 5). The physically more complicated 1965 Stratford production used simple elements to suggest a world that inter-acted and changed around the characters, with four free-standing rectangular blocks 'noiselessly interlocking and sliding apart' to suggest houses, windows and walls.[24] Clearly following a thematic conception of the play's world, the 1975 Marlowe Society pro-duction offered 'a series of platforms at different levels, "fenced" with jagged slabs of gold' which left the characters 'forever climb-ing precarious-looking ladders, and conversing with each other from positions of isolation'.[25]

THE PLAY

Although the title of the 1633 quarto is *The Famous Tragedy of the Rich Jew of Malta*, by the time of its first modern revival in 1818 Marlowe's play was neither famous nor – as written – considered tragic.[26] The fact that one hundred years later the play's most influential modern critical assessor, T.S. Eliot, also refused it the name of tragedy suggests a problem for con-sideration.[27] In neither case was the issue simply the play's abun-dance of humour. There were also the perceived difficulties posed by that humour's object as well as by its nature. Already in Kean's revival of 1818, there is evident concern about how to

---

[23] *The Sunday Times*, 18 March 1984; *RORD* 28 (1985), 165

[24] *The Times*, 17 April 1965

[25] *RORD* 18 (1975), 61–2

[26] See Smith, 'The Jew of Malta', on Kean's performance.

[27] Eliot's remarks are from 'Christopher Marlowe' in *Selected Essays* (New York, 1964).

relate the play's representation of that transhistorical object of anti-Semitism the 'rich Jew', who, as the prologue claims, 'smiles to see how full his bags are crammed', to the philosophical weight and dignity demanded of tragedy. To address this difficulty, Kean's production took two major steps. A new prologue was substituted for the original, disclaiming any sectarian intention to 'cast opprobrium o'er the Hebrew name' and asserting the play's moral universality: 'On every sect pernicious passions fall, / And vice and virtue reign alike in all'.[28] Secondly, the play – in particular its last two acts – was revised in order that Barabas be given greater dignity as a victim.

Eliot's influential critical assessment of the play, a judgement that continues to influence critics and players alike, also denies Marlowe's play the status of tragedy. Taking his cue from a reading of the play's final acts, the portion modified most heavily in Kean's stage version, Eliot assesses *The Jew of Malta* 'not as a tragedy', nor even as an instance of the 'tragedy of blood', that violent and popular Elizabethan revenge genre, but as a 'farce' of 'terribly serious, even savage comic humour'. Subsequent criticism and stage production have continued to respond, whether explicitly or not, to the issues that concern these pioneering instances of production and critical interpretation.

Whatever their limitations, Kean's revision in the interests of dignity and universality and Eliot's redefinition of genre for purposes of revaluation both point to important features of Marlowe's play. Eliot's recognition of the play's savage comedy in particular is obviously valid. Whether it is Barabas taking extravagant delight in the deaths of his victims –

> There is no music to a Christian's knell:
> How sweet the bells ring now the nuns are dead
> That sound at other times like tinkers' pans!   (IV.i.1–3)

– or invoking familiar proverbs while committing mayhem –

BERNARDINE
> What do you mean to strangle me?

ITHAMORE
> Yes, 'cause you use to confess.

BARABAS
> Blame not us but the proverb, 'Confess and be hanged'.
> Pull hard.   (IV.i.144–7)

– or providing an aside to remind the audience, as he so often does, of a homicidal intention lurking beneath his high moral rhetoric –

[28] Smith, 'The Jew of Malta', p. 7

As these have spoke so be it to their souls.
(I hope the poisoned flowers will work anon.)   (V.i.42–3)

– there is a high proportion of such juxtaposed humour and physical violence. But Eliot also calls the play 'serious'. What makes its comedy truly 'serious' is not the dire effects of its physical violence but the conceptual assaults that are directed as much against the values and opinions of the audience as against the characters themselves.

There may be, as Eliot suggests, a savage quality to the play's humour, but, as the discipline of anthropology has taught us, what appears 'savage' to one culture or group may be, upon further inspection, more a matter of difference than of brutality or primitiveness. The play may differ from classical standards of high tragedy, whether that genre be defined by Aristotle, Sir Philip Sidney or Eliot, yet it is so much more than mere farce, sick comedy or crude racism because of its relentless ironies. The ironic potential of a dramatic world where intention and strategy repeatedly come to unexpected, often catastrophic conclusions (e.g. Barabas's plans to conceal his wealth, to have his daughter feign conversion to Catholicism, to employ Ithamore against his enemies, to profit from Ferneze's captivity, etc.) is compounded by reiterated key terms (e.g. 'policy', 'profession'); by frequent and often wildly misappropriated allusions (e.g. Ithamore's ridiculous botch of Marlowe's own 'Come live with me' or Barabas's distortions of proverbial and biblical sources); and by an extensive, innovative use of asides. A clearer sense of what all this might amount to emerges if the play is seen not against some timeless, essential definition of the tragic but in relation to the various forms of the tragic that it evokes, as well as in relation to the institutions, concerns and discourses important to London of the 1590s – its theatre, religion and politics.

Marlowe's 'famous' play, arguably the most popular theatre piece of the 1590s, repeatedly suggests alternative forms of tragedy, even as it embodies something rather different from any of them. As Barabas is warned by Friar Jacomo, one might hear the possibility of a tragedy resembling Sophocles' *Oedipus Rex*, when the arrogant assurance of King Oedipus, who will not see his own errors, conflicts with the knowledge of the literally blind prophet Teiresias, who sees the source of Theban pollution all too clearly:

JACOMO
    Barabas, although thou art in misbelief,
    And wilt not see thine own afflictions,
    Yet let thy daughter be no longer blind.

BARABAS

    Blind, friar? I reck not thy persuasions.   (I.ii.349–52)

One obvious difficulty with this model, of course, lies in the utter unsuitability of Friar Jacomo – or anyone else in Marlowe's play – to assume, as Teiresias does, the voice of rectitude. Amid their pious platitudes, the official spokesmen of Christianity eagerly violate every Christian tenet with their own greed, lust, violence and lying. If the Sophoclean model of tragedy, of wilful self-blind-ness forced into confrontation with uncompromising knowledge, is not adequate, then neither is another tragic form that is evoked by the violent seizure of Barabas's property for the good of the state. The lines of Barabas and Ferneze may suggest the potential of a tragic encounter between mutually exclusive 'rights' like that embodied in the contests of Creon and Antigone in Sophocles' *Antigone* (which had recently been translated by Marlowe's associ-ate Thomas Watson)[29] –

FERNEZE

    Content thee, Barabas, thou hast nought but right.

BARABAS

    Your extreme right does me exceeding wrong: (I.ii.153–4)

– but the 'right' of the Maltese community is here represented as no more clear and uncompromised than any other standard suggested by the play. It is rather a matter of dubious inter-national 'policy' – the Turks having allowed the Maltese debt to accumulate in order to justify an assertion of imperial domination (I.i.180ff.) – and brutal domestic economic exploitation – the Maltese authorities using the Jews as a convenient source of revenue.

    Closer in time and culture than any classical model, the 'tragic' Tudor narratives concerning the falls of princes provide another possible unifying pattern. So Barabas bewails the inevitable effects of mutability in lines that recall lamentations from *The Mirror for Magistrates*:

    The incertain pleasures of swift-footed time
    Have ta'en their flight, and left me in despair;
    And of my former riches rests no more
    But bare remembrance; like a soldier's scar,
    That has no further comfort for his maim.   (II.i.7–11)

But this is all an act. The lament is only part of one of Barabas's multiple schemes rather than a genuine expression of his own miserable condition or that of the world in general.

---

[29] Watson's translation is licensed in 1581 (Eccles, *Christopher Marlowe in London*, pp. 129–31).

The play's opening moments strongly recall Marlowe's own recently staged and vastly successful tragedy of the 'overreacher' *Tamburlaine*.[30] Like Tamburlaine, Barabas – played by the same Edward Alleyn who had acted the role of Tamburlaine – opens his tragedy with images of enormous aspiration, to 'inclose / Infinite riches in a little room' (I.i.36–7). Yet such rhapsodic ambition quickly gives way to plots, schemes and poisonings that have little or nothing to do with anything beyond personal grievances. However, there are two more apposite tragic models for the play's construction: the Tudor homiletic tragedy, with which the innovative second part of Marlowe's own *Tamburlaine* had recently experimented, and the Kydian revenge tragedy, which had itself just burst upon the theatrical scene.

The Jew of Malta frequently shares lines and passages with Kyd's enormously popular *Spanish Tragedy*, but the relationship goes well beyond mere verbal borrowing to more fundamental similarities and, ultimately, differences. Like the tragedies of Seneca, Kyd's play and Marlowe's open with a supernatural frame, dramatize the pursuit of violent revenge and indulge in extreme emotional rhetoric; but four innovative features of the Kydian form deserve mention as contributions to *The Jew of Malta*: its representation of social tensions, its deployment of multiple ironies, its interrelation of heroism and villainy and its use of humour.

What is new about Kyd's version of Senecan form is above all the remarkable degree to which tragedy is rendered in concretely social terms. The action is framed by ghosts and demons concerned with fulfilment of their own bloody vengeance, as Seneca's plays had been, but the agonies of the protagonist and his victims are constructed and inflected within recognizable Elizabethan social tensions. Kyd's Hieronimo is arguably the first tragic protagonist to live and die amid the constraints of a middling condition.[31] Hieronimo has to get up and go to work, despite his tragic sufferings, and fulfil responsibilities in a world where status, money and education are significant factors that shape, channel and impinge upon desires, actions and language. Such material-social considerations are not part of the Senecan inheritance. Nor, for that matter, does Seneca develop as strongly the ethical-metaphysical tensions that mark Kyd's half-Christian dramatic universe. Despite all its supernatural machinery, *The*

---

[30] The most complete discussion of Marlowe's works in these terms is Harry Levin's *The Overreacher: A Study of Christopher Marlowe* (Cambridge, Mass., 1952); recent studies have disputed the application of Levin's terms to *The Jew of Malta*.
[31] On Kyd's middling protagonist, with observations concerning the relation of Kyd and Marlowe, see James R. Siemon, 'Sporting Kyd', *ELR* 24 (1994), 553–582.

Spanish Tragedy repeatedly suggests that however much an audience might sympathize with him, Hieronimo's successes as a revenger must also be evaluated against multiple ironies. These ironies are registered verbally, in brief biblical allusions to the injunction against revenge or in the confusions of action that dog the revenge itself, as when a well-meaning bystander (the Duke of Castile) and a revenger herself (Bel-Imperia) alike fall victim to seemingly indiscriminate slaughter. And they are evident in intonations which suggest the costs of vengeance to the capacity for judgement: the ghost, for example, who had started the play as a victim with very little thought of revenge, closes it so enraptured by the very fact of violence that his triumphant epilogue indiscriminately hails both the violent acts that achieve his revenge and those that destroy his friends as 'spectacles to please my soul' (IV.v.12). What this means, in practice, is that Kydian tragedy develops an implicit similarity between villainy and heroism. The machinations of its innately cruel villain mirror those of its increasingly cruel protagonist. Finally, its action unfolds in an atmosphere marked by pervasive grotesque humour concerning such otherwise 'tragic' matters as life and death, justice and morality (for example in Hieronimo's eating the pleas of the commoners for justice). Against these characteristic features of Kydian tragedy one may detect the similarities and differences that mark Marlowe's treatment of the Kydian inheritance.

Hieronimo is Spanish and Catholic; Barabas is like him in belonging to a publicly detested religious and ethnic category – Jew in his case – and yet also like him in acquiring the potential for audience sympathy through suffering an obvious injustice perpetrated by those who possess social and political authority. Both begin their plays with labours and aspirations defined in terms of a 'profession', and against the backdrop of other conflicts and alliances both international and erotic, both come to neglect their professions to pursue revenge. Through repeated setbacks and frustrations, they achieve elaborate successes before finally falling victim in their own moments of triumph. Yet their differences are profound.

Obvious differences lie in Barabas's unabashed materialism, his self-acknowledged egocentrism and his immediate, excessive pursuit of revenge. Without provocation Barabas professes an indiscriminate readiness to sacrifice Christian and Jew alike: 'Nay, let 'em combat, conquer, and kill all, / So they spare me, my daughter, and my wealth' (I.i.151–2). And it is 'wealth' that he cares about, rather than some more acceptably universal value like Hieronimo's commitment to justice.[32] Barabas explicitly

[32] Erich Segal points out that Barabas echoes the self-definition of Envy – 'I am Envy

rejects the claims of such values as 'conscience', 'faith' and 'principality', while reinterpreting the biblical 'blessings promised to the Jews' as material 'plenty', and approving its pursuit in imagery that, as N.W. Bawcutt has suggested, ironically echoes Ovid's descriptions of the cruel Age of Iron.[33] When he does suffer loss of any sort – in finances, in real property, in control over his daughter's heart or her religious convictions – he repays it, not with proportionate response, but with murder, even mass murder. Furthermore, the very first time the audience is asked to sympathize with him in ways that recall the claims made upon us by the agonies of Hieronimo, Barabas does something Hieronimo never does: he deceives us. As his subsequent scornful denunciations of his on-stage sympathizers reveal, his passionate actions are mere tricks:

> See the simplicity of these base slaves,
> Who for the villains have no wit themselves,
> Think me to be a senseless lump of clay
> That will with every water wash to dirt:
> No, Barabas is born to better chance,
> And framed of finer mould than common men,
> That measure nought but by the present time.
> A reaching thought will search his deepest wits,
> And cast with cunning for the time to come:
> For evils are apt to happen every day.   (I.ii.216–25)

By implication, as David Bevington says, this revelation of hypocrisy ridicules us as 'common men' for having been cheated into 'misplaced sympathy'.[34] And as Robert C. Jones has argued, after the experience of this first encounter, an audience is likely to be stung by Barabas's taunts about 'simplicity' and lack of 'wit' into an alienated resolve 'not to trust Barabas and not, by all means, to pity him again'.[35] However, we might also be likely, as Jones maintains, to laugh at him – not just with him but at

---

... O that there would come a famine through all the world, that all might die, and I live alone' (*Dr Faustus* V.303–7) – in his own proclamation – 'For so I live, perish may all the world' (V.v.10); see 'Marlowe's *Schadenfreude*: Barabas as Comic Hero', in Harry Levin, ed., *Veins of Humor* (Cambridge, Mass., 1972), pp. 69–92 (p. 84).

[33] See Bawcutt's edition, p. 21.

[34] Bevington, *Mankind to Marlowe*, p. 225

[35] *Engagement with Knavery: Point of View in Richard III, The Jew of Malta, Volpone and The Revenger's Tragedy* (Durham, N.C., 1986); contrast Jones's sense of audience alienation with assertions of audience identification with Barabas by Stephen Greenblatt ('Marlowe, Marx, and Anti-Semitism' in *Learning to Curse: Essays in Early Modern Culture* (New York, 1990), pp. 40–58, (esp. pp. 50–1)); James L. Simmons

him – when his self-proclaimed superiority of wit and foresight deserts him, as it so frequently will and even as it does in this very instant of triumph. No sooner has Barabas congratulated himself on his 'reaching thought' than he learns that his plans have been thwarted by Governor Ferneze's seizure of his hidden treasure, prompting another outbreak of cursing and lamentation, this time unfeigned and unpitied (I.ii.258–65).

The ironic rhythm of such boastful contrivance, limited success and subsequent laughable difficulty is an old one on the English stage. Barabas's last boast to us is clearly derived from the overconfident braggart villains and vices of earlier drama – 'Now tell me, worldlings, underneath the sun, / If greater falsehood ever has been done' (V.v.49–50) – and its predictable outcome seems to endorse an archaic dramaturgy and cosmology.[36] His death in a boiling 'cauldron' would appear designed to lend itself to the moralizing typical of the Tudor hybrid homiletic drama, and Ferneze's pitiless final pronouncements on the providential role of 'heaven' in safeguarding the Christian community against Barabas's 'unhallowed deeds' fit this pattern. But does Marlowe's drama endorse this final say by an antagonist who has appropriated the evildoer's own treacherous means and machinery while heaping religious and racial abuse upon him?

The Jew of Malta is not Marlowe's first play to represent cunning caught in its own devices amid reflections on the justice of divine Providence, nor is it his first play to situate this conjunction within a multicultural setting. The Sigismund episodes of *Tamburlaine II* conform to similarly homiletic contours and concern antagonists divided by religion and race.

Anticipating a threat from the 'heathenish Turks and pagans' (II.i.6) who are currently their allies, the Christian forces of *Tamburlaine II* violate their oaths of peace, suffer the consequences and experience a tragic recognition. The Christian decision concludes an extended verbal struggle in which key terms of sixteenth-century religious and political discourse are enlisted to overcome the scruples of the debaters about profaning

---

('Elizabethan Stage Practice and Marlowe's *Jew of Malta*', *RenD* 4 (1971), 93–104, esp. pp. 103–4); and, at greatest length, J.B. Steane (*Marlowe: A Critical Study* (Cambridge, 1974), esp. p. 172, where Barabas is called our 'entertainer').

[36] The most extended discussion of the relation of the play to the morality play and its Vice figures is in Bernard Spivack, *Shakespeare and the Allegory of Evil: The History of a Metaphor in Relation to His Major Villains* (New York, 1958), esp. pp. 346–55. Spivack says of this speech: 'The waning life of the allegorical stage revives intensely in such a speech: in its didactic and demonstrative principle, its ironic inversion of the homiletic point, its rallying impeachment of the audience, its celebration of deceit' (p. 351).

the 'grace of our profession' (II.i.32). The key terms in these debates are religious 'profession' and worldly 'policy', and a central assumption is that of Christian Providence – the divine ordering principle proclaimed by Elizabethan orthodoxy to be evident in historical circumstances. Because Muslims are 'infidels', it is argued, they cannot be trusted, so to keep a promise to them is to violate 'necessary policy', that widely, if uneasily, recognized demand of sixteenth-century statecraft which, since Machiavelli, had posited self-interest as a universal rule of political conduct.[37] Secondly, observing an oath with these Muslims is called 'sinful' because circumstances suggest a Providential 'opportunity' to act on God's behalf against their 'blasphemous paganism'. However, the play represents these arguments in ways that render them suspect: any Protestant might recognize in circumstances where policy is preferred to profession, and opportunity to oath, obvious similarities to notorious instances of Roman Catholic treachery, while any churchgoer might detect the supporting biblical precedents to be misappropriated.[38]

Certain elements of the recently staged *Tamburlaine II* are obviously relevant to the ethnic and religious conflict in *The Jew of Malta*. Not only do both plays represent European Christianity encountering a non-Christian Other, but they are similarly concerned with the interaction of religious 'profession' and worldly 'policy'. This association is stressed from the first lines of the Prologue – spoken by the sixteenth-century embodiment of politic thinking, the spirit of Niccolò Machiavelli, and emphasizing the politics of religious vocation – and in the reiterated word 'policy' (thirteen occurrences as against only six instances in all of Marlowe's other works, often in tandem with 'profession' – as in Barabas's compact denunciation of Christian hypocrisy: 'Ay, policy? that's their profession, / And not simplicity, as they suggest' (I.ii.161–2)).[39] Furthermore, there are important similarities in dramatic action linking *The Jew of Malta* and the Sigismund episodes.

---

[37] On 'policy', see N.W. Bawcutt, ' "Policy", Machiavellianism, and the Earlier Tudor Drama', *ELR* 1 (1971), 195–209; also Howard S. Babb, 'Policy in Marlowe's *Jew of Malta*', *ELH* 24 (1957), 85–94.

[38] On the sources and significance of the Sigismund–Orcanes story of *Tamburlaine II*, especially its relationships to notorious cases of Catholic oath breaking, see Roy W. Battenhouse, 'Protestant Apologetics and the Subplot of *2 Tamburlaine*', *ELR* 3 (1973), 30–43. For casuistry as a divisive religious issue during the period, see Edmund Leites, ed., *Conscience and Casuistry in Early Modern Europe* (Cambridge, 1988).

[39] Word frequency counts from Charles Crawford, *The Marlowe Concordance* (Louvain, 1911–32) are given in Bawcutt's edition, p. 54.

The Christians of *Tamburlaine II* conclude their debates with a pious-sounding resolution to surprise 'the pagan, / And take the victory our God hath given', but their mortal defeat occasions a recognition that what had been called 'necessary policy' was actually a 'sin' of 'hateful perjury'. Even the treatment of the Muslims, who might be expected to embody 'foul blasphemous paganism' for a European Christian audience,[40] supports the ascendancy of this moral; for, in contrast to the treacherous, partisan Christians, the victorious Muslims are ecumenical universalists who invoke Christ as well as Mohammed and who judge everyone by spiritual standards:

> Can there be such deceit in Christians,
> Or treason in the fleshly heart of man,
> Whose shape is figure of the highest God? (II.ii.36–8)

This may be surprising, yet there is no missing its universalizing moral: 'deceit' is bad no matter how it may be supported by discourses of politic self-interest, ethno-centrism or religious prejudice – even one's own. But consider the difference between the humanist moral absolutes of this attack on treachery and prejudice and Marlowe's complicated presentation of the seizure of Barabas's wealth and the death of his daughter, Abigail.

Abigail enters the play expressing justifiable pity for her father, undertakes redress of his 'wrongs', becomes herself enmeshed in 'policy' and suffers the mortal consequences, only to conclude by piously repenting her errors. Abigail's final self-accounting exemplifies tragic *anagnoresis* or recognition, defined in decidedly Christian terms:

> I was chained to follies of the world:
> But now experience, purchasèd with grief,
> Has made me see the difference of things.
> My sinful soul, alas, hath paced too long
> The fatal labyrinth of misbelief,
> Far from the Son that gives eternal life. (III.iii.62–7)

---

[40] For example, during the siege of Malta in 1565 prayers are appointed to be read, beseeching God to defend the island against 'the rage and violence of Infidels, who, by all tyranny and cruelty labour utterly to root out not only true Religion, but also the very name and memory of Christ our only Saviour, and all Christianity' (cited in G.K. Hunter, 'The Theology of Marlowe's *The Jew of Malta*', *JWCI* 27 (1964), 211–40 (p. 229)). Queen Elizabeth refers to the Turks in 1596 as 'the common enemy of Christ' (G.B. Harrison, ed., *The Letters of Queen Elizabeth* (London, 1935), p. 243); compare the Duke's reference in *Othello* to 'the general enemy Ottoman' (I.iii.51). On the other hand, both England and France had ties and offered aid to the Ottomans in the sixteenth century, enlisting the Sultan as a counterweight to Spanish and German Habsburg power (see Carl Max Kortepeter, *Ottoman Imperialism During the Refor*

Painful 'experience' is said to have clarified a 'difference' between the falsity of worldly illusion and the certainty of Christian dogma, with its promise to the believer of a better, truer world to come.

The content of this speech may be orthodox enough, but that this edifying and Christian end should come to this particular character, and in the specific circumstances that accompany it, is deeply ironic. The 'difference', after all, that has prompted Abigail's recognition is not merely a metaphysical difference between the folly of this world and the certainties of the next, but a grossly prejudiced distinction between races and religions: 'But I perceive there is no love on earth, / Pity in Jews, nor piety in Turks' (III.iii.49–50). Abigail, who is herself a Jew, alone of all the play's characters expresses pity and has felt love for both father and fiancé. That she should betray her very virtues in so prejudiced an expression is extremely ironic and suggests a confusion that goes beyond the convert's passion. But that Abigail would be prompted by such ethnic-religious misrecognitions to commit herself into the keeping of Malta's grossly hypocritical friars, as if they embodied a true Christian love, pity and piety, is too plainly ironic to be missed by any audience. Lest one miss the point, her dying profession, imploring Friar Bernardine to 'witness that I die a Christian', is answered by a comic rejoinder that makes a leering mockery of love, pity and piety: 'Ay, and a virgin too, that grieves me most' (III.vi.41).

Why does the play give such prominence to abuses by professed Christians? Is this part of an attempt at even-handedness like that suggested in Kean's moral universalism? If Barabas is greedy, violent and hypocritical, so are the friars. Does the play suggest a universal economic determinism? The Bashaw presumes that 'all the world' is driven by 'Desire of gold' (III.v.3–4). Barabas claims that none is 'honoured now but for his wealth' (I.i.112), and such diverse practices as statecraft, religion, sex and even poetry are implicated in economic pursuit. Certainly, the scene (II.iii) that combines Christian slave trading (with 'every one's price written on his back'), Lodowick's negotiating of the 'price' of Abigail's affection, Katherine's evaluating which slave is 'comeliest' and Barabas's purchase of Ithamore powerfully reinforces this idea of a world where all relationships are understood in material terms. Yet concentration on any such single moral or standard of moral evaluation is not only out of place for a play

mation: Europe and the Caucasus (New York, 1972), pp. 1–2). For an excellent account of the play within the dynamics of imperialism, see Emily C. Bartels, *Spectacles of Strangeness: Imperialism, Alienation and Marlowe* (Philadelphia, 1993).

in which multiple moral issues are repeatedly, in T. W. Craik's phrase, 'ironically touched upon and left', but it could short-circuit a fuller understanding of those ironic touches them-selves.[41] After all, in the very scene in which this economic factor seems omnipresent, Barabas dismisses his costly defrauding by an unnamed merchant with a jaunty 'I have wealth enough' and returns to the pursuit of a revenge that – often to his economic cost – dominates his attention.

What is innovative about *The Jew of Malta* is not that it depicts a world driven by any single viciousness that is especially concentrated in any single Vice figure – old plays like Preston's *Cambyses* had done that – or that its characters are depicted individually violating clear-cut abstract standards of ethical behaviour, but that their practices and perceptions are so often complicated – as is Abigail's own conversion – by distorted misrecognitions that are themselves formed, articulated and sup-ported socially. The same 'vice and virtue' do not 'reign alike in all'; rather vices and virtues, like the mistakes that accompany them, are represented as specific to institutions and situations. The play's pervasive ironies constantly remind one of this fact.

However much the characters – Jew, Turk, Christian – manage to suggest a resemblance to one another and, ultimately, to Barabas in their diverse histories of wrongdoing, pretence and miscalculation, they are also differentiated according to occu-pation or role. As an imperial lord, Calymath assumes that it is 'more kingly to obtain by peace / Than to enforce conditions by constraint' (I.ii.25–6), trusts in the strategy of spying that his delay necessitates and pays with the loss of everything. As head of government, Ferneze lets the Maltese tribute lapse (I.ii), cunningly reinterprets his mistake as 'Honour[able]' resistance when offered Spanish support (II.ii) and suffers all but total defeat and humiliation. As a victorious admiral, Del Bosco mis-takenly tries to sell Turks in Malta, cleverly recasts his marketing problem in terms of a unified defence of the honour of 'Christen-dom' (II.ii), but proves unable to produce a Spanish might to match that of the Turks. As spiritual confessor, Friar Bernardine violates the 'canon law' concerning confessional sanctity (III.vi) to blackmail Barabas, but somehow mistakenly believes that he can trust a confession extorted from Barabas (IV.i) and is killed. Cunningly violating his professions of love for Mathias, Lodow-ick believes he can credit Barabas's and Abigail's own feigned professions of love (II.iii) and pays with his life. These manifest

---

[41] See Craik's edition, p. xiv; cf. Constance Brown Kuriyama, *Hammer or Anvil: Psychological Patterns in Christopher Marlowe's Plays* (New Brunswick, N.J., 1980), on Malta as a world of 'universal lust for self gratification' (p. 171).

instances of error and violation are related to social categories – ruler, admiral, priest, lover – as is the equally self-defeating duplicity undertaken by the play's courtesan, pickpocket and Turkish slave against their client, associate and master. And he humorously epitomizes the relation of specific vices to specific roles in his famous boasts about multiple careers. Barabas studied medicine, only to facilitate 'dead men's knells'; he became a military engineer as a 'pretence' by which to slay 'friend and enemy'; as a usurer, he delighted in 'extorting, cozening, forfeiting, / And tricks belonging unto brokery' (II.iii.176–203). But with these very boasts of his cunning, Barabas ironically forms an alliance that will prove disastrous. Dull-witted Ithamore proves smart enough to give the cunning misanthrope of all trades a very difficult time.

Of course circumstances of social definition are important whenever Barabas is involved, since he embodies a contradictory position defined by the distinction of being the *rich* Jew of Malta and by the odium of being the rich *Jew* of Malta.[42] Through Barabas the play focuses attention on the diverse ways ethnic and religious identity may enter into behaviour, business practices, communal affiliation, family affection, physical demeanour, wealth and cleverness. Sometimes Barabas's pronouncements may be simply understood as calculated anticipations of the prejudices of others rather than revealing his own views. Thus, it makes sense that Barabas resorts to ethnic terms to explain Abigail's weeping upon the occasion of her coerced engagement: ' 'tis the Hebrews' guise, / That maidens new betrothed should weep a while' (II.iii.328–9). Similarly, he chooses to 'dissemble' a confession to commonplace Christian accusations of 'Jewish' partisan zealotry, pitilessness, greed, usury, wealth and hypocrisy:

> I have been zealous in the Jewish faith,
> Hard-hearted to the poor, a covetous wretch,
> That would for lucre's sake have sold my soul.
> A hundred for a hundred I have ta'en;
> And now for store of wealth may I compare
> With all the Jews in Malta; but what is wealth?
> I am a Jew, and therefore am I lost. (IV.i.51–7)

But other statements are not so easily understood as merely

---

[42] For anti-Semitic discourse generally, cf. note 10 above; for Elizabethan treatments of Jewishness as symbolic of failings in Christianity, see Alan C. Dessen, 'The Elizabethan Stage Jew and Christian Example: Gerontus, Barabas, and Shylock', *MLQ* 35 (1974), 231–45; cf. Hunter; Kocher, *Christopher Marlowe*; and Katz, *Philo-Semitism* (esp. p. 162).

calculated. The very sight of Lodowick apparently arouses vis-
ceral revulsion in Barabas, Lodowick's shaven face – like 'a hog's
cheek new singed' (II.iii.43) – embodying difference from Jewish
standards of diet and countenance. Moreover, Barabas's sol-
iloquies revel privately in his success at constructing, for the
benefit of Christians, their own stereotyped images of the Jew:

> We Jews can fawn like spaniels when we please;
> And when we grin we bite, yet are our looks
> As innocent and harmless as a lamb's.
> I learned in Florence how to kiss my hand,
> Heave up my shoulders when they call me dog,
> And duck as low as any bare-foot friar,
> Hoping to see them starve upon a stall,
> Or else be gathered for in our synagogue;
> That when the offering-basin comes to me,
> Even for charity I may spit into't. (II.iii.20–9)

In a related vein, Barabas's advice to Abigail urges her to deceive
Lodowick 'like a cunning Jew' (II.iii.238). What should we make
of a play that gives lines like these to a Jewish speaker? The
expropriation of Barabas's wealth illustrates the play's complex
treatment of anti-Semitism.

The Maltese officials, like Abigail, are hostile to Jews, but,
unlike her, they calmly invoke impeccable authority rather than
confused personal experience. Echoing polemic ultimately
derived from the Bible (Matthew 32), Ferneze calls Jews 'infidels
... accursed in the sight of heaven' for the guilt which is attributed
to them collectively in accounts of the crucifixion of Christ.
Thus, the seizure of Barabas's wealth may be articulated as a
divinely ordained punishment for this 'inherent' guilt:

> If your first curse fall heavy on thy head,
> And make thee poor and scorned of all the world,
> 'Tis not our fault, but thy inherent sin. (I.ii.108–10)

Furthermore, with equally impeccable authority derived from
contemporary Elizabethan state discourse, the Maltese officials
reason that their political misfortune – the tribute demanded by
the Turks – is a Providential punishment for their sin of religious
tolerance. Thus, Ferneze says, it is 'through our sufferance of
your hateful lives ... These taxes and afflictions are befallen'
(I.ii.63–5).[43]

[43] Compare the charges of 1601 against one of the Earl of Essex's co-conspirators, Sir
Christopher Blunt, for seeking 'toleration of religion' (William Cobbett, *Complete
Collection of State Trials* (London, 1809), vol. 1, pp. 1421–2). Alexander Ross claims
that 'Diversity of *Religions* beget envy, malice, seditions, factions, rebellions, contempt

However orthodox, this religiously sanctioned extortion – historically accurate in depicting European taxation of the Jewish community – occurs within an atmosphere charged with suspicion that religious profession might mask secret political manoeuvring.[44] Before the event, Barabas warns us to beware Christian 'malice, falsehood, and excessive pride' unfitting their 'profession' (I.i.116–17); during the seizure, he demands of the Christians, 'Bring you scripture to confirm your wrongs?' (I.ii.111); and afterwards he defines their tactics as strategy masked by righteous language: 'policy? that's their profession, / And not simplicity, as they suggest' (I.ii.161–2). Secondly, the play grants its victimized Jew an ethically powerful and biblically derived response to his antagonists. Barabas answers the imputation of racial guilt by asserting individual moral responsibility in phrases that echo the praise of righteousness in Proverbs 10 ('The treasures of wickednes profite nothing: but righteousness delivereth from death'):

> But say the tribe that I descended of
> Were all in general cast away for sin,
> Shall I be tried by their transgression?
> The man that dealeth righteously shall live:
> And which of you can charge me otherwise? (I.ii.114–18)

Finally, the play vitiates the Christian claims with internal ironies of form and allusion. In the persecution of Barabas there are many reminders of the Bible's account of Christ's passion. Ferneze echoes the notoriously hypocritical utterances of the officials who expedite the crucifixion. From Caiaphas's justification of the persecution of Christ, Marlowe derives Ferneze's claim 'better one want for a common good, / Than many perish for a private man' (I.ii.99–100; cf. John 11:50); and from Pilate's self-exculpation Marlowe takes Ferneze's image of handwashing, 'Barabas, to stain our hands with blood / Is far from us and our profession' (I.ii.145–6; cf. Matthew 27:24).[45] The professed Christians re-enact the persecution of Christ, as Ferneze answers Barabas's impassioned claim of righteousness: 'Excess of wealth

---

of Superiours, treacheries, innovations, disobedience, and many more mischiefs, which pull down the heavy judgements of God upon that State or Kingdom, where contrary *Religions* are allowed' ([*Pansebeia*] *Or, A View of all Religions in the World* (London, 4th ed., 1664)).

[44] On treatment of the Jews as, in effect, 'indirect tax-collectors', see Pollins, *Economic History*, p. 19; for similar treatment of Protestant 'strangers' see Pettegree, *Foreign Protestant Communities*, p. 294.

[45] On the notoriety of John 11:50 and its complex uses in arguments about the mysteries of state, see Peter S. Donaldson, *Machiavelli and Mystery of State* (Cambridge, 1988), p. 175.

is cause of covetousness: / And covetousness, oh 'tis a monstrous sin' (I.ii.124–5). Ferneze's hypocrisy in preaching on the evils of wealth while seizing someone's property is registered by the form of his utterance, his pious maxim rendered unctuous and suspect by its extra-metrical 'oh'.

Thus far, the play's treatment of conflict between Jew and Christian resembles the ethical critique of Christian worldly practice in *Tamburlaine II*. But even if criticism of Christianity is an important feature of *The Jew of Malta*, the play as a whole reaches beyond theology to remind its Elizabethan audience of other conflicts outside the theatre, connecting Barabas to concerns about a group thought to share occupations and values, if not religion, with Jews – the Machiavellian merchant 'strangers'.

If sixteenth-century London had no openly practising Jews, it had, nevertheless, its own marginal group – the resident community of Protestant 'strangers' mainly from France and the Netherlands – who could and did provide a focus for sometimes violent animosities.[46] These fears and resentments of fellow European Protestants are articulated in terms – economic, religious, behavioural – that resemble those of historical anti-Semitism and that are remarkably like the charges that could be made against Barabas.[47]

Like Barabas himself, these charges comprise a monstrosity of fears and resentments about attitudes, practices and associations that are seen infecting every level and aspect of society. Strangers are reputed both to be subservient to powers of state and to harbour revolutionary desires, to be both religiously hypocritical and fanatical, to collude in spying for domestic authorities and to be complicit with the aims of foreign enemies. They are said to forge links with the lower orders and dubious ties to the nobility; they are guilty of the labourless exploitation of usury and the ambitious pursuit of multiple trades. These combinations of abuses are perhaps most interesting in two articulations concerning politics, economics and spectacle. The same merchant figure who is associated with a standard Tudor litany of disapproved economic practices – usury, engrossing, forestalling, unauthorized retailing – is also defined in terms of a political doctrine that had no economic component – Machiavellianism – and in the language of contemporary anti-theatrical discourse – 'with his horrible showes' he 'Vndoeth thowsands'.

There are historical and geographical explanations for the charges of Machiavellianism. Since Gentillet it had become com-

---

[46] On this subject see Pettegree, *Foreign Protestant Communities*; also Archer, *The Pursuit of Stability*, esp. pp. 131–48.

[47] See appendix below (pp. 115–18) for an example of the relevant discourse.

monplace to associate France with Machiavellian politics, while Huguenot resistance to authority had made them widely suspect, despite their credentials as Protestants.[48] Thus, whatever their remove from the exalted reaches of statecraft, there might be an understandable association of Continental immigrants with the popular image of Machiavelli as legitimating amoral self-interest. On the other hand, there was a felt distrust of the dimly understood, but much denounced, practices and values of an emergent capitalism.[49]

However, among all the other resonances of the charges against strangers with the person and career of Barabas, none seems to me so fraught with potential interest for a consideration of the play as the charge that the merchant stranger threatens the well-being of the community with 'horrible showes'. The parts of *The Jew of Malta* that have most troubled the critics, after all, have been – as they are in *Doctor Faustus* – those portions in which the fulfilment of the play's initial tragic impetus in a 'moral' conclusion is delayed by elaborate, sometimes apparently gratuitous shows: the 'delud[ing]' of the amorous Lodowick with shows of love (II.iii); the 'cunningly performed' (II.iii.369) duel that entraps the lovers and prompts Ithamore's appreciation for being 'So neatly plotted, and so well performed' (III.iii.2); Barabas's 'dissemble[d]' conversion (IV.i.47); the framing of Friar Jacomo with the artfully disposed corpse of Friar Bernardine (IV.i); Barabas's performance 'in some disguise' (IV.iii.66) as a French musician bearing poisoned flowers (IV.iv); and the faking of his death (V.i). Perhaps it is something analogous to this substitution of manner for matter, of diverting contrivance for solid content, of 'gawds' for 'goods', of Mephistophilis' 'shows' for true omniscience, that is suspect in the marketing practices – and even in the more highly wrought goods themselves – associated with the strangers.[50]

---

[48] See J.H.M. Salmon, *The French Religious Wars in English Political Thought* (Oxford, 1959). In Marlowe's youth, Canterbury was a centre of violent religious factionalism and of Huguenot immigration (Peter Clark, 'Josias Nicholls and Religious Radicalism, 1553–1639', *Journal of Ecclesiastical History* 28 (1977), 133–50).

[49] See Marx's chapters on 'So-called Primitive Accumulation' and on English agricultural expropriation in vol. 2 of *Capital*. Also of interest in a consideration of *The Jew of Malta* are chapters 20 and 36 of vol. 3, in which the 'twin brothers' – merchant capital and usurer's capital – are analysed as forms of capital preceding capitalist modes of production (New York, 1981). Compare the analysis of the early modern 'reconceptualization of economic life' in Joyce Oldham Appleby, *Economic Thought and Ideology in Seventeenth-Century England* (Princeton, 1978).

[50] On the development of a market for such goods, see Joan Thirsk, *Economic Policy and Projects: The Development of a Consumer Society in Early Modern England* (Oxford, 1978). For marketing and theatre-like deception, compare the complaint of *A manifest*

Barabas himself constantly tries to anticipate the demands of the Maltese community. Despite some brilliant successes – especially his supply of confessions to fulfil the friars' conceptions of what it means to be 'zealous in the Jewish faith' (IV.i.28–80) – the frequency of his asides marks virtually every utterance of his as a conscious labour of strategic distortion. He attempts, in Machevill's phrase, to 'guard' his true values from his tongue and market himself successfully. Even his confessions of thinking 'like a cunning Jew' appear strategic – telling the truth with as much attention to situation as if it were a lie.[51]

Thus, it seems to be in keeping with his practice that Barabas proclaims the moral equivalence and strategic superiority of conscious individual hypocrisy over the community's unthinking entrapment in social rituals:

> As good dissemble that thou never mean'st
> As first mean truth and then dissemble it;
> A counterfeit profession is better
> Than unseen hypocrisy. (I.ii.290–3)

Yet when it comes to assessing how well Barabas has really done in pursuing his self-professed method of turning counterfeit shows of agreement or compliance to use in 'Making a profit of ... policy' (V.ii.112), the results are hardly positive. The 'business' of statecraft (V.ii.110) depends, as does the 'policy' of economic life, on forces beyond the power of the isolated individual strategist – no matter how demonic in energy, ruthless in analysis or proficient in counterfeiting. Over and over again, self-serving schemes come to 'unseen' conclusions owing to overlapping and interlocking circumstances of an emotional, economic, religious and political nature. One might call the effects of this larger field of conditions, alliances and discourses the work of 'heaven', as does Ferneze in the play's final line, but in the light of its pitiless workings, this name might seem a misrecognition of something else.

That something else might be called by names that Ferneze rejects: 'fate' or 'fortune', the one pertaining to the causality of classical tragedy and the other to the perverse chance against

---

detection of the most vyle and detestable use of Diceplay (1552): 'Could merchants, without lies, false making their wares, and selling them by a crooked light, to deceive the chapman in the thread or colour, grow so soon rich and to a baron's possessions, and make all their posterity gentlemen?' (in Gamini Salgādo, ed., *Cony Catchers and Bawdy Baskets* (Harmondsworth, 1972), p. 43). For a recent account of Marlowe's complex relation to anti-theatricalism, see Debra Belt, 'Anti-Theatricalism and Rhetoric in Marlowe's *Edward II*', *ELR* 21 (1991), 134–65.

[51] Cf. Emily Bartels, *Spectacles of Strangeness*, on Barabas 'strategically play[ing] the Jew'.

which Machiavelli's agents must contend in order to win power and glory. Yet, in the light of the crucial role played by the play's strategists themselves in their own undoing, one might resist these attempts at explanation. One might instead consider Marlowe's play as suggesting through its paradoxes an intellectual space that would later come be to occupied by the concept of ideology, that internalization of the 'unseen' social determinants of human discourse and epistemology.[52] The self-deceiving process by which Barabas falls resembles that which levels Faustus, Marlowe's other protagonist who is notably too smart, and not smart enough, for his own good. Like Machevill, both Barabas and Faustus condescend to 'petty wits' who rest content within social limitations instead of pursuing the independence of policy or magic. Yet neither can escape values assumed by the social order they reject, Faustus oddly affirming 'resolut[ion]' in 'manly fortitude' (V.6; III.86) over the evidence of his own senses, Barabas stupidly choosing 'profit' over 'authority' (V.ii.27–46), under the orthodox, but patently illusory, assumption that 'peaceful rule [with] Christians kings' (I.i.133) will prove better for him than the continuation of a state of war.

This drama of half-swallowed asides and incompleted sentences, of grotesquely hypocritical rhetoric, of grossly hyperbolic violence, of pervasive, cynical economic motivation and of religious and ethnic resentments has no clear successors in Marlowe's own brief canon. The twentieth century needs no lessons in hatred and prejudice, to be sure, nor any help from sensational drama to foster brutality and cynicism. But in a post-modern world grown increasingly transnational in economics and in lived experience, one may regret the lack of further Marlovian exploration in the social vein opened by *The Jew of Malta*.[53] The play's potential to disturb the unspoken 'doxa' of its own social order suggests no small risk for its first producers.[54] The risk of modern theatrical production is that, deprived of its Elizabethan contexts and thereby of many of its multiple ironies, the play's

[52] Bob Hodge offers a useful account of ideology in the play (see note 14 above); for a good introduction to current debates about the nature of ideology, see Terry Eagleton, *Ideology: An Introduction* (London, 1991).
[53] On transnationalism and tribalism, see John F. Stack, ed., *Ethnic Identities in a Transnational World* (Westport, Ct., 1981), esp. pp. 18–36; cf. Fredric Jameson on post-modern group consciousness (*Postmodernism or, the Cultural Logic of Late Capitalism* (Durham, N.C., 1991), esp. pp. 346–8).
[54] 'Doxa' is Pierre Bourdieu's term for the 'undisputed, pre-reflexive, naive, native compliance with the fundamental presuppositions' of a culture or one of its sub-fields; it is an unspoken 'unanimity effect' produced by that which, within the confines of culture or group, literally goes without saying (*The Logic of Practice* (Stanford, 1990), p. 68).

nightmare representation of anti-Semitism's hated object will constitute encouragement of prejudice. This danger is a factor to be reckoned with in the play's modern stage history.

THE TEXT

Although *The Jew of Malta* was entered in the Stationers' Register for 17 May 1594, the only early text is the 1633 quarto published by Nicholas Vavasour and printed in the shop of John Beale (I.B.). I have chiefly used the Bodleian Library copy (shelf mark Mal. 172 [2]), consulting as well copies from the British Library (shelf mark 82.c.22 [5]) and the Houghton Library (shelf mark 14416.35.15). In addition, I have compared the modern editions of N.W. Bawcutt (The Revels Plays, 1978), H.S. Bennett (*The Jew of Malta and The Massacre at Paris*, 1931), Fredson Bowers (*The Complete Works of Christopher Marlowe*, 1981), T.W. Craik (New Mermaids, 1966), R.A. Fraser (*Drama of the English Renaissance*, 1976), J.B. Steane (*The Complete Plays of Christopher Marlowe*, 1969) and R.W. Van Fossen (Regents Renaissance Drama, 1964).

It has been argued – largely on the basis of perceived disunity of style and tone – that the quarto reflects an extensive revision, probably by Thomas Heywood; but studies of vocabulary, spelling, metre and dramaturgy have generally supported the now widely held opinion that the quarto derives from some version of a Marlovian original.[55] While exhibiting numerous trivial printing errors, the quarto text presents few serious difficulties of language, plot or speech attribution requiring editorial emendation. Such features as its inconsistency in speech prefixes (often these are generic, but not consistently so: e.g. Barabas is *Iew* in I.i. and elsewhere *Bar.*; Friar Jacomo is *1 Fry.* except in IV.i., where he is *Ioco.*) and character names (e.g. Ithamore is usually Ithimore, sometimes Ithimer), coupled with its frequent omission of entries, exits and important stage directions, have lent support to the theory that the text is derived from a relatively clean copy of authorial 'foul papers' rather than from theatrical prompt copy. If the manuscript was obviously in the possession of the actors, its difficulties in such basic mechanical features argue against their having acted from it.

The early text is divided into acts, but not into scenes, which, following general practice, have been added for the present edition. Spelling has been modernized, but, mindful of Ethel Seaton's observations on the potential implications of punc-

[55] See Bawcutt, pp. 39–46.

tuation for interpretation and delivery in other Marlovian texts –
especially the frequently used colon – I have kept the punctuation
of the original wherever it did not seem to present serious difficulty of comprehension.[56] Lineation is frequently a problem in
the quarto text, with many instances of what appear to be the
printers' relineation of prose as verse lines beginning with capital
letters (e.g. IV.ii.43–6; V.i.32–4). Changes in lineation have been
noted. The exceptionally extensive use of asides in the play
presents difficulties, since the precise beginning and end points
of the individual aside are sometimes unclear (e.g. I.i.172).
Occasionally the text couples the use of italics with the direction
'aside' to indicate the extent of the aside (e.g. II.iii.83), but since
this typographical convention is not consistently observed, I have
not adopted it, though its appearance in the original is noted in
relevant passages. Asides are marked in the present edition by
parentheses. For cases in which characters are having a conversation aside with one another, one set of parentheses encloses
the entire conversation (e.g. IV.iv.23–4); otherwise separate sets
of parentheses are employed for each aside. Editorial additions,
except those noted in the footnotes, have been included in square
brackets. The abbreviation 'ed.' refers to emendation by any
editor.

[56] Ethel Seaton, 'Marlowe's Map', *Essays and Studies* 10 (1924), 31–2

FURTHER READING

Bartels, Emily C., ed., *Critical Essays on Christopher Marlowe* (New York, 1997)

Bartels, Emily C., 'Malta, the Jew, and the Fictions of Difference: Colonialist Discourse in Marlowe's *The Jew of Malta'*, *ELR* 20 (1990), 1–16

   Spectacles of Strangeness: Imperialism, Alienation and Marlowe (Philadelphia, 1993)

Bawcutt, N.W., 'Machiavelli and Marlowe's *The Jew of Malta'*, *RenD* n.s. 3 (1970), 3–49

Bevington, David, *From Mankind to Marlowe; Growth of Structure in the Popular Drama of Tudor England* (Cambridge, Mass., 1962)

Cartelli, Thomas, *Marlowe, Shakespeare and the Economy of Theatrical Experience* (Philadelphia, 1991)

Cheney, Patrick, *Marlowe's Counterfeit Profession: Ovid, Spenser, Counter-nationhood* (Toronto, 1997)

Deats, Sara Munson and Lisa S. Starks, ' "So Neatly Plotted, and So Well Perform'd": Villain as Playwright in Marlowe's *The Jew of Malta'*, *TJ* 44 (1992), 375–89

Dessen, Alan C., 'The Elizabethan Stage Jew and Christian Example: Gerontus, Barabas, and Shylock', *MLQ* 35 (1974), 231–45

Friedenreich, Kenneth, Roma Gill and Constance B. Kuriyama, *'A Poet and a filthy Play-maker': New Essays on Christopher Marlowe* (New York, 1988)

Goldberg, Dena, 'Sacrifice in Marlowe's *The Jew of Malta, SEL* 32 (1992), 233–45

Grantley, Darryll and Peter Roberts, eds., *Christopher Marlowe and English Renaissance Culture* (Hants, 1996)

Greenblatt, Stephen, 'Marlowe, Marx, and Anti-Semitism', in *Learning to Curse: Essays in Early Modern Culture* (New York, 1990)

Healey, Thomas, *Christopher Marlowe* (Plymouth, 1994)

Hodge, Bob, 'Marlowe, Marx, and Machiavelli; Reading into the Past', in David Aers et al., eds, *Literature, Language and Society in England, 1580–1680* (Dublin, 1981)

Hunter, G. K., 'The Theology of Marlowe's *The Jew of Malta'*, *JWCI* 27 (1964), 211–40

Jones, Robert C., *Engagement with Knavery; Point of View in Richard III, The Jew of Malta, Volpone and The Revenger's Tragedy* (Durham, N.C., 1986)

Kocher, Paul H., *Christopher Marlowe: A Study of His Thought, Learning and Character* (New York, 1946)

Levin, Harry, *The Overreacher: A Study of Christopher Marlowe* (Cambridge, Mass., 1952)

McAdam, Ian, 'Carnal Identity in *The Jew of Malta*', *ELR* 26 (1996), 46–74

Maclure, Millar, ed., *Marlowe: The Critical Heritage 1588–1896* (London, 1979)

Maguin, Jean-Marie, '*The Jew of Malta:* Marlowe's Ideological Stance and the Playworld's Ethos', *CE* 27 (1985), 17–26

Minshull, Catherine, 'Marlowe's "Sound Machevill" ', *RenD* 13 (1982), 35–53

Palmer, Daryl W., 'Merchants and Miscegenation: *The Three Ladies of London, The Jew of Malta* and *The Merchant of Venice*', in Joyce MacDonald, ed., *Race Ethnicity, and Power in the Renaissance* (Madison, NJ, 1997)

Rothstein, Eric, 'Structure as Meaning in *The Jew of Malta*', *JEGP* 65 (1966), 260–73

Sales, Roger, *Christopher Marlowe* (New York, 1991)

Shapiro, James, *Rival Playwrights: Marlowe, Jonson, and Shakespeare* (New York, 1991)

Shapiro, James, *Shakespeare and the Jews* (New York, 1996)

Shepherd, Simon, *Marlowe and the Politics of Elizabethan Theatre* (Brighton, 1986)

Smith, James L., '*The Jew of Malta* in the Theatre', in Brian Morris, ed., Christopher Marlowe (London, 1968)

Tambling, Jeremy, 'Abigail's Party: "The Difference of Things" in *The Jew of Malta* in Dorothea Kehler and Susan Baker, eds., *In Another Country: Feminist Perspectives on Renaissance Drama* (Metuchen, NJ, 1991)

Thurn, David H. 'Economic and Ideological Exchange in Marlowe's *Jew of Malta*', *TJ* 46 (1994), 157–70

Weil, Judith, *Christopher Marlowe: Merlin's Prophet* (Cambridge, 1977)

The Famous
TRAGEDY
OF
THE RICH IEVV
OF *MALTA*.

AS IT WAS PLAYD
BEFORE THE KING AND
QVEENE, IN HIS MAJESTIES
Theatre at *White-Hall*, by her Majesties
Servants at the *Cock-pit*.

Written by CHRISTO:HER MARLO.

LONDON;
Printed by *I. B.* for *Nicholas Vavasour*, and are to be sold
at his Shop in the Inner-Temple, neere the
Church. 1633.

THE EPISTLE DEDICATORY

To my worthy friend, Mr. THOMAS HAMMON,
of Gray's Inn, &c.

This play, composed by so worthy an author as Mr Marlo;
and the part of the Jew presented by so unimitable an actor
as Mr. Allin, being in this later age commended to the
stage: as I ushered it unto the Court, and presented it to
the Cock-pit, with these Prologues and Epilogues here   5
inserted, so now being newly brought to the press, I was
loath it should be published without the ornament of an
Epistle; making choice of you unto whom to devote it; than
whom (of all those gentlemen and acquaintance, within
the compass of my long knowledge) there is none more   10
able to tax ignorance, or attribute right to merit. Sir, you
have been pleased to grace some of mine own works with
your courteous patronage; I hope this will not be the worse
accepted, because commended by me; over whom, none
can claim more power or privilege than yourself. I had no   15
better a New-year's gift to present you with; receive it
therefore as a continuance of that inviolable obligement,
by which, he rests still engaged; who as he ever hath, shall
always remain,

Tuissimus:

THO. HEYWOOD.

0.2 *Thomas Hammon* Heywood also dedicated two of his own plays to Hammon
(Part II of *The Fair Maid of the West* (1631) and Part I of *The Iron Age* (1632)).

0.3 *Gray's Inn* one of the Inns of Court; a centre of legal training

3 *Allin* Edward Alleyn (1566–1626), famous actor of the late sixteenth century; he
first acted the roles of Tamburlaine, Faustus and Barabas.

4 *ushered* introduced
Court The title-page asserts that the play was performed 'before the King and
Queen, in his Majesties Theatre at *White-Hall*'.

5 *Cock-pit* located in Drury Lane, one of the two principal Caroline theatres (also
known as The Phoenix)

11 *tax* censure
right just assessment

17 *obligement* obligation

20 *Tuissimus* (Latin) wholly yours

THE PROLOGUE TO THE STAGE,
AT THE COCK-PIT

We know not how our play may pass this stage,
But by the best of *poets in that age   *Marlo
The Malta Jew had being, and was made;
And he, then by the best of †actors played: †Allin
In *Hero and Leander*, one did gain   5
A lasting memory: in *Tamburlaine*,
This *Jew*, with others many: th' other wan
The attribute of peerless, being a man
Whom we may rank with (doing no one wrong)
Proteus for shapes, and Roscius for a tongue,   10
So could he speak, so vary; nor is't hate
To merit in ‡him who doth personate   ‡Perkins
Our Jew this day, nor is it his ambition
To exceed, or equal, being of condition
More modest; this is all that he intends,   15
(And that too, at the urgence of some friends)
To prove his best, and if none here gainsay it,
The part he hath studied, and intends to play it.

4 *Allin* Edward Alleyn. See note to Epistle Dedicatory.
5 *Hero and Leander* Marlowe's erotic narrative poem, based on Musaeus and
  published in 1598
6 *Tamburlaine* Alleyn also played the title role in Marlowe's *Tamburlaine*.
7 *wan* won
10 *Proteus* a sea god of Greek myth with the power of changing shape
   Roscius Quintus Roscius Gallus (d. 62 B.C.), the most famous Roman comic
   actor; later associated with great acting generally
11–12 *hate / To merit* i.e. an expression of jealousy to praise
12 *Perkins* Richard Perkins (d. 1650), a famous actor of the Jacobean and Caroline
   stage, acting c. 1602–37
14 *condition* temperament
16 *urgence* solicitation
17 *prove* try
   gainsay oppose

EPILOGUE

In graving, with Pygmalion to contend;
Or painting, with Apelles; doubtless the end
Must be disgrace: our actor did not so,
He only aimed to go, but not out-go.
Nor think that this day any prize was played,   5
Here were no bets at all, no wagers laid;
All the ambition that his mind doth swell,
Is but to hear from you, (by me) 'twas well.

Epilogue
  1 *graving* sculpture
    Pygmalion the mythic king of Cyprus who fell in love with a beautiful statue he
    made (see Ovid, *Metamorphoses* X); the type of the great artist
  2 *Apelles* a Greek painter (4th century B.C.) of legendary skill
  4 *out-go* surpass
  5 *prize was played* contest was engaged in (from fencing)
  6 *no wagers laid* Apparently bets were sometimes made on the relative merits of
    actors.

THE PROLOGUE SPOKEN AT COURT

Gracious and great, that we so boldly dare,
('Mongst other plays that now in fashion are)
To present this; writ many years agone,
And in that age, thought second unto none;
We humbly crave your pardon: we pursue   5
The story of a rich and famous Jew
Who lived in Malta: you shall find him still,
In all his projects, a sound Machevill;
And that's his character: he that hath past
So many censures, is now come at last   10
To have your princely ears, grace you him; then
You crown the action, and renown the pen.

EPILOGUE

It is our fear (dread Sovereign) we have been
Too tedious; neither can't be less than sin
To wrong your princely patience: if we have,
(Thus low dejected) we your pardon crave:
And if aught here offend your ear or sight,   5
We only act, and speak, what others write.

Prologue
7 *still* always
8 *sound* complete, thorough
Machevill See note on p. 9.
10 *censures* criticisms
Epilogue
1 *dread* revered
2 *can't* can it
4 *Thus low dejected* i.e. bowing

DRAMATIS PERSONAE

MACHEVILL, the Prologue
BARABAS, the Jew of Malta
FERNEZE, the Governor of Malta
ITHAMORE, a Turkish slave to Barabas
SELIM-CALYMATH, the Turkish leader, son of the Turkish
  Emperor
CALLAPINE, a Bashaw
ABIGAIL, the daughter of Barabas
DON LODOWICK, the Governor's son
DON MATHIAS, his friend and lover of Abigail
KATHERINE, the mother of Don Mathias
MARTIN DEL BOSCO, Vice-Admiral of Spain
FRIAR JACOMO
FRIAR BERNARDINE
BELLAMIRA, a courtesan
PILIA-BORZA, a thief in league with her
ABBESS
NUN
Two MERCHANTS; three JEWS; KNIGHTS; BASHAWS; OFFICERS;
SLAVES; CITIZENS; Turkish SOLDIERS; MESSENGER; CARPENTERS

No list of *Dramatis Personae* is given by Q.

THE JEW OF MALTA

PROLOGUE

[Enter] MACHEVILL

MACHEVILL

Albeit the world think Machevill is dead,
Yet was his soul but flown beyond the Alps,
And now the Guise is dead, is come from France
To view this land, and frolic with his friends.
To some perhaps my name is odious,   5
But such as love me, guard me from their tongues,
And let them know that I am Machevill,
And weigh not men, and therefore not men's words:
Admired I am of those that hate me most.
Though some speak openly against my books,   10
Yet will they read me, and thereby attain
To Peter's chair: and when they cast me off,
Are poisoned by my climbing followers.
I count religion but a childish toy,
And hold there is no sin but ignorance.   15
Birds of the air will tell of murders past?

0.2 *Machevill* ed. (Q *Macheuil*); rhyming with 'still' in Heywood's Court Prologue;
    here an embodiment of the spirit of Niccolò Machiavelli, understood as the
    essence of villainous self-interested calculation. The opinions of this stage figure
    diverge significantly from those to be found in Machiavelli's writings, and may
    be indebted to the anti-Machiavellian discourse of writers like Innocent Gentillet
    (see Minshull and Bawcutt).
3 *the Guise* Henri de Lorraine, third Duke of Guise (1550–88), Roman Catholic
    opponent of the Huguenots and, in 1572, director of the St Bartholomew's Day
    massacre (see Marlowe's *Massacre at Paris*)
4 *this land* England (mocking the hope expressed in contemporary polemic (e.g.
    Gentillet) that political calculation would not contaminate England from the
    Continent)
5–6 Meaning unclear: either the devotees of Machiavellianism protect him from
    his critics or, more likely, the disciples follow Machiavelli's precepts while avoiding
    mention of his name.
8 *weigh* esteem   9 Even those who denounce Machiavelli admire him in secret.
12 *Peter's chair* the papacy
14 *toy* trifle. Machiavelli actually took religion seriously as a factor of political
    life (see *Discourses* I.11–15), but his opponents often described his doctrine as
    atheism.
16 *past?* ed. (Q past;)
    Such anecdotes, in which birds reveal an otherwise hidden crime, are taken by

9

I am ashamed to hear such fooleries:
Many will talk of title to a crown.
What right had Caesar to the empire?
Might first made kings, and laws were then most sure   20
When like the Draco's they were writ in blood.
Hence comes it, that a strong built citadel
Commands much more than letters can import:
Which maxima had Phalaris observed,
H'had never bellowed in a brazen bull   25
Of great ones' envy; o'th' poor petty wites,
Let me be envied and not pitied!
But whither am I bound, I come not, I,
To read a lecture here in Britaine,
But to present the tragedy of a Jew,   30
Who smiles to see how full his bags are crammed,
Which money was not got without my means.
I crave but this, grace him as he deserves,
And let him not be entertained the worse
Because he favours me.   35

                                           [*Exit*]

Machevill to exemplify the force of superstition rather than to evidence Providential order.

19 Here Machevill follows Machiavelli, who argues that Caesar was actually little different from the villainous Catiline, but won praise through wealth and power (*Discourses* I.10).

21 *Draco's* ed. (Q *Drancus*) referring to an Athenian legislator of proverbial severity

22 Citadels are traditionally used by tyrants to dominate their subjects (Bawcutt); the value of citadels is ambiguous in Machiavelli: in *The Prince* (XX) they are accorded limited value against internal enemies, but in *Discourses* (II.24) their usefulness is criticized.

23–5 According to legend the Sicilian tyrant Phalaris was killed in the brazen bull he had employed to roast his enemies. The opposition here implied is that between an interest in letters as a weakness and the use of force as a ruler's only true strength.

24 *maxima* ed. (Q maxime) maxim

26 *ones'* ed. (Q ones)
wites either 'wights' (people) or 'wits'

27 *envied . . . not pitied* proverbial (Tilley, E 177)

29 *Britaine* Either 'Britain' or 'Britainy' – apparently the forms were equivalent in Elizabethan usage (cf. *Edward II* II.ii.42).

31 *crammed,* ed. (Q cramb'd)

32 The suggestion that Machiavellian tactics have economic implications is odd, but, as Bawcutt points out, in keeping with Gentillet's polemical version of Machiavellianism.

33 *grace* honour

35 *favours* either 'resembles' or 'sides with'

[Act I, Scene i]

Enter BARABAS *in his counting-house,*
with heaps of gold before him

BARABAS
So that of thus much that return was made:
And of the third part of the Persian ships,
There was the venture summed and satisfied.
As for those Samnites, and the men of Uz,
That bought my Spanish oils, and wines of Greece,   5
Here have I pursed their paltry silverlings.
Fie; what a trouble 'tis to count this trash.
Well fare the Arabians, who so richly pay
The things they traffic for with wedge of gold,
Whereof a man may easily in a day   10
Tell that which may maintain him all his life.
The needy groom that never fingered groat,
Would make a miracle of thus much coin:
But he whose steel-barred coffers are crammed full,
And all his lifetime hath been tired,   15
Wearying his fingers' ends with telling it,
Would in his age be loath to labour so,
And for a pound to sweat himself to death:
Give me the merchants of the Indian mines,
That trade in metal of the purest mould;   20
The wealthy Moor, that in the Eastern rocks

1 *Barabas* ed. (Q *Iew* throughout scene except in stage directions). The name
Barabas is that of the criminal released in place of Jesus (Mark 15.7). This speech
is remarkable for beginning a play in mid-sentence and for the resemblance of
its catalogue of jewels to that found in the opening speech of the Jew Jonathas in
the fifteenth-century Croxton *Play of the Sacrament*.

3 *summed and satisfied* reckoned up and paid off

4 *Samnites* ed. (Q *Samintes*) Central Italian people who fought Rome several times
from 354 B.C. The reference to them combined with that to the biblical Uz (Job
1.1) and, subsequently, to Kirriah Jairim (after a city named in Joshua 15.9;
Judges 18.12) suggests the extent of Barabas's trade, but also his polyglot associations of biblical and classical references and discourses.

6 *silverlings* (Q silverbings) silver coin equivalent to Jewish shekel

8 *well fare* optative phrase: 'Good fortune to them' (cf. V.i.61)
pay ed. (Q pay,)

11 *tell* count

12 *groom* slave, servant
groat coin of small value (cf. IV.ii.117)

Without control can pick his riches up,
And in his house heap pearl like pebble-stones;
Receive them free, and sell them by the weight,
Bags of fiery opals, sapphires, amethysts,   25
Jacinths, hard topaz, grass-green emeralds,
Beauteous rubies, sparkling diamonds,
And seldseen costly stones of so great price,
As one of them indifferently rated,
And of a caract of this quantity,   30
May serve in peril of calamity
To ransom great kings from captivity.
This is the ware wherein consists my wealth:
And thus methinks should men of judgement frame
Their means of traffic from the vulgar trade,   35
And as their wealth increaseth, so inclose
Infinite riches in a little room.
But now how stands the wind?
Into what corner peers my halcyon's bill?
Ha, to the east? Yes: see how stands the vanes?   40
East and by south: why then I hope my ships
I sent for Egypt and the bordering isles
Are gotten up by Nilus' winding banks:
Mine argosy from Alexandria,
Loaden with spice and silks, now under sail,   45
Are smoothly gliding down by Candy shore
To Malta, through our Mediterranean sea.
But who comes here? How now.

22 *without control* without restraint
28 *seldseen* ed. (Q seildsene) seldom seen, rare
29 *rated* valued
30 *caract* ed. (Q Carrect) carat, measure of gem weight, or possibly sign of character
   (cf. *Measure for Measure* V.i.59). This semantic ambiguity of quantity and quality
   is potentially significant in a work with such economic interests and such insistent
   punning.
34 *frame* define, distinguish
37 *Infinite riches in a little room* Hunter defines this as a parody of traditional Christian
   imagery concerning the Virgin Birth; however, the phrase is also proverbial for
   great worth in a humble package (Tilley, W 921).
39 *halcyon* kingfisher, when dead and hung up supposed to act as a weather vane
40 *stands* As frequently in Marlowe, singulars and plurals are interchangeable; cf.
   lines 46 and 109.
44 *argosy* large merchant ship
46 *Candy* Crete
48 *But who comes here?* a formula for dramatic entry already archaic in Marlowe's
   day, but in keeping with some of the other stylistic qualities of the play

Enter a MERCHANT

MERCHANT
  Barabas, thy ships are safe,
  Riding in Malta road: and all the merchants   50
  With other merchandise are safe arrived,
  And have sent me to know whether yourself
  Will come and custom them.
BARABAS
  The ships are safe thou say'st, and richly fraught?
MERCHANT
  They are.
BARABAS   Why then go bid them come ashore,   55
  And bring with them their bills of entry:
  I hope our credit in the custom-house
  Will serve as well as I were present there.
  Go send 'em three score camels, thirty mules,
  And twenty waggons to bring up the ware.   60
  But art thou master in a ship of mine,
  And is thy credit not enough for that?
MERCHANT
  The very custom barely comes to more
  Than many merchants of the town are worth,
  And therefore far exceeds my credit, sir.   65
BARABAS
  Go tell 'em the Jew of Malta sent thee, man:
  Tush, who amongst 'em knows not Barabas?
MERCHANT
  I go.
BARABAS
  So then, there's somewhat come.
  Sirrah, which of my ships art thou master of?   70
MERCHANT
  Of the Speranza, sir.
BARABAS   And saw'st thou not
  Mine argosy at Alexandria?
  Thou couldst not come from Egypt, or by Caire

---

50 *road* ed. (Q Rhode) harbour
53 *custom* see them through customs procedures
54 *fraught* loaded with merchandise
63 *very custom barely* the duties alone
70 *sirrah* a contemptuous form of address
    master of ed. (Q Master off)
71–2 ed. (Q And ... Alexandria? / Thou)
73 *Caire* Cairo

But at the entry there into the sea,
Where Nilus pays his tribute to the main.   75
Thou needs must sail by Alexandria.

MERCHANT

I neither saw them, nor inquired of them.
But this we heard some of our seamen say,
They wondered how you durst with so much wealth
Trust such a crazèd vessel, and so far.   80

BARABAS

Tush; they are wise, I know her and her strength:
But go, go thou thy ways, discharge thy ship,
And bid my factor bring his loading in.

                                    [*Exit* MERCHANT]

And yet I wonder at this argosy.

                    Enter a SECOND MERCHANT

2 MERCHANT

Thine argosy from Alexandria,   85
Know Barabas doth ride in Malta road,
Laden with riches, and exceeding store
Of Persian silks, of gold, and orient pearl.

BARABAS

How chance you came not with those other ships
That sailed by Egypt?

2 MERCHANT   Sir we saw 'em not.   90

BARABAS

Belike they coasted round by Candy shore
About their oils, or other businesses.
But 'twas ill done of you to come so far
Without the aid or conduct of their ships.

2 MERCHANT

Sir, we were wafted by a Spanish fleet   95
That never left us till within a league,
That had the galleys of the Turk in chase.

BARABAS

Oh they were going up to Sicily: well, go
And bid the merchants and my men dispatch
And come ashore, and see the fraught discharged.   100

---

80 *crazèd* unseaworthy
81 *they are wise* sarcastic
82 *But* ed. (Q By)
83 *factor* agent
88 *orient* from the East, brilliant
95 *wafted* escorted

2 MERCHANT
 I go.   *Exit*
BARABAS
 Thus trowls our fortune in by land and sea,
 And thus are we on every side enriched:
 These are the blessings promised to the Jews,
 And herein was old Abram's happiness: 105
 What more may heaven do for earthly man
 Than thus to pour out plenty in their laps,
 Ripping the bowels of the earth for them,
 Making the sea their servant, and the winds
 To drive their substance with successful blasts?   110
 Who hateth me but for my happiness?
 Or who is honoured now but for his wealth?
 Rather had I a Jew be hated thus,
 Than pitied in a Christian poverty:
 For I can see no fruits in all their faith,   115
 But malice, falsehood, and excessive pride,
 Which methinks fits not their profession.
 Happily some hapless man hath conscience,
 And for his conscience lives in beggary.
 They say we are a scattered nation: 120
 I cannot tell, but we have scambled up
 More wealth by far than those that brag of faith.
 There's Kirriah Jairim, the great Jew of Greece,
 Obed in Bairseth, Nones in Portugal,

102 *trowls* rolls in

104–5 This refers to God's covenant with Abraham. This blessing from Genesis 15 is claimed by Christian theologians, who, like Luther, assert that Jews misinterpret the divine blessing by 'applying it only to a carnal blessing, and do great injury to Scripture' (*Commentary on Galatians* (English ed. 1575)); see Hunter on Galatians 3.13–16; cf. II.iii.48. The passage also echoes Ovid's description of the Age of Iron, as Bawcutt points out.

109 *servant* ed. (Q servants) Singulars and plurals are a source of difficulty from line 106 on.   111 *happiness* prosperity

115 *fruits ... faith* common New Testament image (see John 15.1–6; cf. Kocher, pp. 124–5)

117 *profession* religious faith

118 *Happily ... hapless* haply, perhaps some unfortunate

120 *scattered nation* referring to belief that Jewish dispersal reflected God's anger

121 *scambled up* raked together, perhaps rapaciously

123 *Kirriah Jairim* personal name after a biblical city (see 4n.)

124 *Obed* the child of Ruth and Boaz, and ancestor of Jesus, 'notwithstanding', as the Geneva Bible gloss says, that Ruth was 'a Moabite of base condicion, and a stranger from the people of God' (Ruth 1, 'argument')
    Nones a prominent member of the marrano community in London, Dr Hector Nunez

Myself in Malta, some in Italy,   125
Many in France, and wealthy every one:
Ay, wealthier far than any Christian.
I must confess we come not to be kings:
That's not our fault: alas, our number's few,
And crowns come either by succession,   130
Or urged by force; and nothing violent,
Oft have I heard tell, can be permanent.
Give us a peaceful rule, make Christians kings,
That thirst so much for principality.
I have no charge, nor many children,   135
But one sole daughter, whom I hold as dear
As Agamemnon did his Iphigen:
And all I have is hers. But who comes here?

Enter THREE JEWS

1 JEW
  Tush, tell not me 'twas done of policy.
2 JEW
  Come therefore let us go to Barabas;   140
  For he can counsel best in these affairs;
  And here he comes.
BARABAS   Why how now countrymen?
  Why flock you thus to me in multitudes?
  What accident's betided to the Jews?
1 JEW
  A fleet of warlike galleys, Barabas,   145
  Are come from Turkey, and lie in our road:
  And they this day sit in the council-house
  To entertain them and their embassy.
BARABAS
  Why let 'em come, so they come not to war;
  Or let 'em war, so we be conquerors.   150

131–2 *nothing . . . permanent* proverbial (see Gentillet, pp. 13, 200, 316)
134 *principality* rule
135 *charge* responsibility
137 Ironic, since Agamemnon was forced to sacrifice his daughter Iphigenia to obtain a favourable wind for the Greek military expedition against Troy.
139 *policy* cunning politics; often used pejoratively during the Renaissance to refer to Machiavellian deviousness
147 *they* the rulers of Malta

(Nay, let 'em combat, conquer, and kill all,
  So they spare me, my daughter, and my wealth.)
1 JEW
  Were it for confirmation of a league,
  They would not come in warlike manner thus.
2 JEW
  I fear their coming will afflict us all.   155
BARABAS
  Fond men, what dream you of their multitudes?
  What need they treat of peace that are in league?
  The Turks and those of Malta are in league.
  Tut, tut, there is some other matter in't.
1 JEW
  Why, Barabas, they come for peace or war.   160
BARABAS
  Happily for neither, but to pass along
  Towards Venice by the Adriatic Sea;
  With whom they have attempted many times,
  But never could effect their stratagem.
3 JEW
  And very wisely said, it may be so.   165
2 JEW
  But there's a meeting in the senate-house,
  And all the Jews in Malta must be there.
BARABAS
  Umh; all the Jews in Malta must be there?
  Ay, like enough, why then let every man
  Provide him, and be there for fashion-sake.   170
  If any thing shall there concern our state
  Assure yourselves I'll look (unto myself).
1 JEW
  I know you will; well brethren let us go.

---

151 ed. (Q has a marginal '*aside*') This is the first of Barabas's many lines spoken
    only in part to his on-stage interlocutors. The precise limits of the aside portions
    of his lines are often ambiguous; however, very often it appears that they are the
    final words or phrases, which serve to modify or contradict what precedes them.
    Asides are marked in the present edition by parentheses.

156 *Fond* foolish

163 *With whom* against whom

168 *Umh* a noise indicating reflectiveness

170 *provide him ... for fashion-sake* get ready ... according to form

171 *our state* the material conditions of Jews or their collective standing as a defined
    class or group

172 ed. (Q has a marginal '*aside*')

2 JEW

Let's take our leaves; farewell good Barabas.

BARABAS

Do so; farewell Zaareth, farewell Temainte.   175

[Exeunt JEWS]

And Barabas now search this secret out.
Summon thy senses, call thy wits together:
These silly men mistake the matter clean.
Long to the Turk did Malta contribute;
Which tribute all in policy, I fear,   180
The Turks have let increase to such a sum,
As all the wealth of Malta cannot pay;
And now by that advantage thinks, belike,
To seize upon the town: ay, that he seeks.
Howe'er the world go, I'll make sure for one,   185
And seek in time to intercept the worst,
Warily guarding that which I ha' got.
Ego mihimet sum semper proximus.
Why let 'em enter, let 'em take the town.   [*Exit*]

[Act I, Scene ii]

Enter [FERNEZE,] GOVERNOR *of Malta,* KNIGHTS [*and*
OFFICERS,] *met by* BASHAWS *of the Turk;* CALYMATH

FERNEZE

Now bashaws, what demand you at our hands?

BASHAW

Know knights of Malta, that we came from Rhodes,
From Cyprus, Candy, and those other isles
That lie betwixt the Mediterranean seas.

---

175 *Temainte* perhaps a reminiscence of Eliphaz the Temanite, one of Job's comforters (Job 2)

178 *silly* simple, innocent
    clean completely

188 *Ego ... proximus* adapted from Terence's *Andria*, '*Proximus sum egomet mihi*' (IV.i.12), 'I am always nearest to myself'

   0.1 GOVERNOR Throughout this scene (e.g. lines 10, 17, 32) Q uses the plural, while the speech heading for the speaker who leads the Maltese Knights is 'Governor'. As in the case of 'Iew' in I.i, a general designation is subsequently replaced with a proper name; by II.ii the leader of Malta is 'Ferneze'.
     BASHAWS ed. (Q BASSOES) pashas, Turkish military functionaries

   4 *seas* The Adriatic, Aegean, etc. Many editors insert a dash here for Q's full stop to reinforce the idea that Ferneze interrupts the Bashaw's oratory.

FERNEZE
  What's Cyprus, Candy, and those other isles   5
  To us, or Malta? What at our hands demand ye?
CALYMATH
  The ten years' tribute that remains unpaid.
FERNEZE
  Alas, my lord, the sum is over-great,
  I hope your highness will consider us.
CALYMATH
  I wish, grave Governor, 'twere in my power   10
  To favour you, but 'tis my father's cause,
  Wherein I may not, nay I dare not dally.
FERNEZE
  Then give us leave, great Selim-Calymath.
CALYMATH
  Stand all aside, and let the knights determine,
  And send to keep our galleys under sail,   15
  For happily we shall not tarry here:
  Now Governor how are you resolved?
FERNEZE
  Thus: since your hard conditions are such
  That you will needs have ten years' tribute past,
  We may have time to make collection   20
  Amongst the inhabitants of Malta for't.
BASHAW
  That's more than is in our commission.
CALYMATH
  What Callapine a little courtesy.
  Let's know their time, perhaps it is not long;
  And 'tis more kingly to obtain by peace   25
  Than to enforce conditions by constraint.
  What respite ask you Governor?
FERNEZE   But a month.
CALYMATH
  We grant a month, but see you keep your promise.
  Now launch our galleys back again to sea,
  Where we'll attend the respite you have ta'en,   30

---

  9 *consider* be considerate of
 10 *grave* worthy of respect
    Governor, ed. (Q Governors)
 13 *give us leave* allow us private conference
    Selim-Calymath Selim was the name of the son of Suleiman the Magnificent,
    Turkish ruler during the seige of Malta in 1565.
 17 *how ... resolved?* What have you decided?
 22 *than ... commission* than we are authorized to do

And for the money send our messenger.
Farewell great Governor, and brave knights of Malta.
Exeunt [CALYMATH *and* BASHAWS]
FERNEZE
And all good fortune wait on Calymath.
Go one and call those Jews of Malta hither:
Were they not summoned to appear today?   35
OFFICER
They were, my lord, and here they come.

Enter BARABAS *and* THREE JEWS

1 KNIGHT
Have you determined what to say to them?
FERNEZE
Yes, give me leave, and Hebrews now come near.
From the Emperor of Turkey is arrived
Great Selim-Calymath, his highness' son,   40
To levy of us ten years' tribute past,
Now then here know that it concerneth us:
BARABAS
Then good my lord, to keep your quiet still,
Your Lordship shall do well to let them have it.
FERNEZE
Soft Barabas, there's more longs to't than so.   45
To what this ten years' tribute will amount,
That we have cast, but cannot compass it
By reason of the wars, that robbed our store;
And therefore are we to request your aid.
BARABAS
Alas, my Lord, we are no soldiers: 50
And what's our aid against so great a prince?
1 KNIGHT
Tut, Jew, we know thou art no soldier;
Thou art a merchant, and a moneyed man,
And 'tis thy money, Barabas, we seek.
BARABAS
How, my lord, my money?

---

35 *today?* ed. (Q to day.)
42 Q's punctuation is a colon, which Ethel Seaton argues ('Marlowe's Map', *Essays and Studies* 10 (1924)) may signal 'rhetorical upward intonation' (p. 31); thus it may be suggested that Barabas interrupts Ferneze before he has completed his statement (cf. line 58).
45 *longs* belongs, pertains
46 *amount,* ed. (Q amount)
47 *cast ... compass* calculated but cannot satisfy

FERNEZE   Thine and the rest.   55
  For to be short, amongst you't must be had.
1 JEW
  Alas, my lord, the most of us are poor!
FERNEZE
  Then let the rich increase your portions:
BARABAS
  Are strangers with your tribute to be taxed?
2 KNIGHT
  Have strangers leave with us to get their wealth?   60
  Then let them with us contribute.
BARABAS
  How, equally?
FERNEZE   No, Jew, like infidels.
  For through our sufferance of your hateful lives,
  Who stand accursèd in the sight of heaven,
  These taxes and afflictions are befallen,   65
  And therefore thus we are determinèd;
  Read there the articles of our decrees.
OFFICER [*reading*]
  First, the tribute money of the Turks shall all be levied
  amongst the Jews, and each of them to pay one half of
  his estate.   70
BARABAS
  How, half his estate? I hope you mean not mine.
FERNEZE
  Read on.
OFFICER [*reading*]
  Secondly, he that denies to pay, shall straight become a
  Christian.
BARABAS
  How, a Christian? Hum, what's here to do?   75
OFFICER [*reading*]
  Lastly, he that denies this, shall absolutely lose all he
  has.
ALL 3 JEWS
  Oh my lord we will give half.

57 *1 Jew* ed. (Q *Iew*)
59 *strangers* foreigners
64 *accursed* i.e. for a role in the Crucifixion of Christ (cf. Matthew 27.25, and line
    108)
68 OFFICER [*reading*] ed. (Q *Reader* as at lines 73, 76)
68–70 ed. (Q First ... be / Leuyed ... one / Halfe ... estate.)
71 Many editors make all or part of this and line 75 asides.
73–4 ed. (Q Secondly ... become / A Christian.)
76–7 ed. (Q *one line*)

BARABAS

   Oh earth-metalled villains, and no Hebrews born!
   And will you basely thus submit yourselves   80
   To leave your goods to their arbitrament?

FERNEZE

   Why Barabas wilt thou be christened?

BARABAS

   No, Governor, I will be no convertite.

FERNEZE

   Then pay thy half.

BARABAS

   Why know you what you did by this device?   85
   Half of my substance is a city's wealth.
   Governor, it was not got so easily;
   Nor will I part so slightly therewithal.

FERNEZE

   Sir, half is the penalty of our decree,
   Either pay that, or we will seize on all.   90

BARABAS

   Corpo di Dio; stay, you shall have half,
   Let me be used but as my brethren are.

FERNEZE

   No, Jew, thou hast denied the articles,
   And now it cannot be recalled.

                          [*Exeunt* OFFICERS]

BARABAS

   Will you then steal my goods?   95
   Is theft the ground of your religion?

FERNEZE

   No, Jew, we take particularly thine
   To save the ruin of a multitude:
   And better one want for a common good,
   Than many perish for a private man: 100
   Yet Barabas we will not banish thee,
   But here in Malta, where thou got'st thy wealth,
   Live still; and if thou canst, get more.

79 *earth-metalled* base, dull in temperament
81 *arbitrament* disposal
85 Craik suggests an echo of Christ's 'They knowe not what thei do' (Luke 23.34).
88 *slightly* easily, without resistance
91 *Corpo di Dio* (Italian) Body of God!
94 Many editors have the officers exit here to seize Barabas's wealth; they apparently
   re-enter at line 131.
96 *ground* basis
99–100 Hunter suggests an echo of John 11.50.
   private individual

BARABAS

   Christians; what, or how can I multiply?

   Of nought is nothing made.   105

1 KNIGHT

   From nought at first thou cam'st to little wealth,

   From little unto more, from more to most:

   If your first curse fall heavy on thy head,

   And make thee poor and scorned of all the world,

   'Tis not our fault, but thy inherent sin.   110

BARABAS

   What? Bring you scripture to confirm your wrongs?

   Preach me not out of my possessions.

   Some Jews are wicked, as all Christians are:

   But say the tribe that I descended of

   Were all in general cast away for sin,   115

   Shall I be tried by their transgression?

   The man that dealeth righteously shall live:

   And which of you can charge me otherwise?

FERNEZE

   Out wretched Barabas,

   Sham'st thou not thus to justify thyself,   120

   As if we knew not thy profession?

   If thou rely upon thy righteousness,

   Be patient and thy riches will increase.

   Excess of wealth is cause of covetousness:

   And covetousness, oh 'tis a monstrous sin.   125

BARABAS

   Ay, but theft is worse: tush, take not from me then,

   For that is theft; and if you rob me thus,

   I must be forced to steal and compass more.

1 KNIGHT

   Grave Governor, list not to his exclaims:

   Convert his mansion to a nunnery,   130

---

105 proverbial; but also potentially a point of contention between Aristotelian and biblical thinking concerning Creation

108 *your first curse* i.e. that of the Jews (cf. line 64)

    thy The shift in pronouns suggests a move from the racially general ('your') to the individual.

113 *as all Christians are* possibly an aside

117 Cf. Proverbs 10.2 ('The treasures of wickednes profite nothing: but righteousnes deliuereth from death') and 12.28.

119–22 ed. (Q Out ... thus / To ... not / Thy ... righteousnesse,)

    Out an expression of reproach

121 *profession* religious creed (cf. line 146), personal code or occupation – i.e. as merchant or as usurer

129 *exclaims* exclamations

Enter OFFICERS

His house will harbour many holy nuns.

FERNEZE

It shall be so: now officers, have you done?

OFFICER

Ay, my lord, we have seized upon the goods
And wares of Barabas, which being valued
Amount to more than all the wealth in Malta.   135
And of the other we have seizèd half.
Then we'll take order for the residue.

BARABAS

Well then my lord, say, are you satisfied?
You have my goods, my money, and my wealth,
My ships, my store, and all that I enjoyed;   140
And having all, you can request no more;
Unless your unrelenting flinty hearts
Suppress all pity in your stony breasts,
And now shall move you to bereave my life.

FERNEZE

No, Barabas, to stain our hands with blood   145
Is far from us and our profession.

BARABAS

Why, I esteem the injury far less,
To take the lives of miserable men,
Than be the causers of their misery.
You have my wealth, the labour of my life,   150
The comfort of mine age, my children's hope,
And therefore ne'er distinguish of the wrong.

FERNEZE

Content thee, Barabas, thou hast nought but right.

BARABAS

Your extreme right does me exceeding wrong:
But take it to you i' the devil's name.   155

FERNEZE

Come, let us in, and gather of these goods

---

136 *the other* the other Jews
137 *the residue* the balance of the tribute or the rest of the affair
146 *profession* Christian principles (cf. line 121)
147 *Why,* ed. (Q Why)
150 *wealth,* ed. (Q wealth)
152 *distinguish of the wrong* draw false distinctions between murder and theft
153 *nought but right* nothing but justice
154 proverbial (Tilley, R 122), but also, of course, a potential nexus for one version
      of classical tragedy
155 *i'the* ed. (Q i'th')

The money for this tribute of the Turk.
1 KNIGHT
   'Tis necessary that be looked unto:
   For if we break our day, we break the league,
   And that will prove but simple policy.   160
                Exeunt [all except BARABAS *and* JEWS]
BARABAS
   Ay, policy? that's their profession,
   And not simplicity, as they suggest.   [*Kneels*]
   The plagues of Egypt, and the curse of heaven,
   Earth's barrenness, and all men's hatred
   Inflict upon them, thou great *Primus Motor*.   165
   And here upon my knees, striking the earth,
   I ban their souls to everlasting pains
   And extreme tortures of the fiery deep,
   That thus have dealt with me in my distress.
1 JEW
   Oh yet be patient, gentle Barabas.   170
BARABAS
   Oh silly brethren, born to see this day!
   Why stand you thus unmoved with my laments?
   Why weep you not to think upon my wrongs?
   Why pine not I, and die in this distress?
1 JEW
   Why, Barabas, as hardly can we brook   175
   The cruel handling of ourselves in this:
   Thou seest they have taken half our goods.
BARABAS
   Why did you yield to their extortion?
   You were a multitude, and I but one,

160 *simple policy* foolish strategy
161–2 *Ay, policy? . . . simplicity* Picking up the phrase 'simple policy', Barabas offers
    an analysis of the hypocrisy of the Maltese Christians, who profess Christian
    honesty – 'the simplicitie that is in Christ' (II Corinthians 11.3) – but practise
    cunning strategy.
162 *Kneels* Barabas is clearly on his knees by line 166 and probably refers to his
    posture at line 172. His kneeling is one of this scene's many echoes of the
    dramaturgy of *The Spanish Tragedy*. The point at which he rises is not clear, but
    Bawcutt's suggestion of line 215 makes sense.
165 *Primus Motor* (Latin) First Mover, 'The chiefest God' of *I Tamburlaine* IV.ii.8–9
    and Aristotle's *Metaphysics*
167 *ban* curse
171 *silly* foolish
172–4 As Craik points out, the patterned repetition of these lines resembles stylistic
    devices of *The Spanish Tragedy;* see also III.iii.46–8 and III. v.35–6.
175 *brook* endure

And of me only have they taken all.   180

1 JEW

Yet brother Barabas remember Job.

BARABAS

What tell you me of Job? I wot his wealth
Was written thus: he had seven thousand sheep,
Three thousand camels, and two hundred yoke
Of labouring oxen, and five hundred   185
She-asses: but for every one of those,
Had they been valued at indifferent rate,
I had at home, and in mine argosy
And other ships that came from Egypt last,
As much as would have bought his beasts and him,   190
And yet have kept enough to live upon;
So that not he, but I may curse the day,
Thy fatal birthday, forlorn Barabas;
And henceforth wish for an eternal night,
That clouds of darkness may enclose my flesh,   195
And hide these extreme sorrows from mine eyes:
For only I have toiled to inherit here
The months of vanity and loss of time,
And painful nights have been appointed me.

2 JEW

Good Barabas be patient.   200

BARABAS

Ay, I pray leave me in my patience.
You that were ne'er possessed of wealth, are pleased
    with want.
But give him liberty at least to mourn,
That in a field amidst his enemies,
Doth see his soldiers slain, himself disarmed,   205
And knows no means of his recovery:
Ay, let me sorrow for this sudden chance;

---

182 *wot* know
182–208 These lines frequently echo chapters 1, 3 and 7 of the Book of Job. Lines
    192–6 are very closely related to Job 3.1–10: 'Afterward Iob opened his mouthe,
    and cursed his day. And Iob cryed out, and said, Let the daye perish, wherein I
    was borne, and the night when it was said, There is a manchilde conceiued. Let
    that day be darkenes, let not God regarde it from aboue, nether let the light shine
    vpon it, But let darkenes, & the shadowe of death staine it: let the cloude remaine
    vpon it, & let them make it feareful as a bitter day ... Because it shut not vp the
    dores of my mothers wombe: nor hid sorowe from mine eyes.' Similarly close
    relationships exist in lines 197–9 to Job 7.3 and in line 208 to Job 7.11.
187 *at indifferent rate* impartially evaluated
201 *Ay, I* ed. (Q I, I)

'Tis in the trouble of my spirit I speak;
Great injuries are not so soon forgot.
1 JEW
  Come, let us leave him in his ireful mood,   210
  Our words will but increase his ecstasy.
2 JEW
  On then: but trust me 'tis a misery
  To see a man in such affliction:
  Farewell Barabas.

                                        Exeunt [JEWS]
BARABAS
  Ay, fare you well.   215
  See the simplicity of these base slaves,
  Who for the villains have no wit themselves,
  Think me to be a senseless lump of clay
  That will with every water wash to dirt:
  No, Barabas is born to better chance,   220
  And framed of finer mould than common men,
  That measure nought but by the present time.
  A reaching thought will search his deepest wits,
  And cast with cunning for the time to come:
  For evils are apt to happen every day.   225
  But whither wends my beauteous Abigail?

            Enter ABIGAIL *the Jew's daughter*

  Oh what has made my lovely daughter sad?
  What? woman, moan not for a little loss:
  Thy father has enough in store for thee.
ABIGAIL
  Not for myself, but agèd Barabas: 230
  Father, for thee lamenteth Abigail:
  But I will learn to leave these fruitless tears,
  And urged thereto with my afflictions,
  With fierce exclaims run to the senate-house,
  And in the senate reprehend them all,   235

---

210 *ireful* enraged

211 *ecstasy* passion

216–17 *simplicity ... base slaves ... villains* Barabas changes tone abruptly, con-
    descending to the departed Jews as foolish, socially inferior and debased generally.

219 *with every water wash to dirt* fall into disarray at any sort of trouble

220 *chance* fortune

223 *reaching thought* penetrating analyst

224 *cast with cunning* wisely anticipate

226 *Abigail* On the association of the biblical Abigail (I Samuel 25) with conversion
    to Christianity, see Hunter, p. 225.

And rent their hearts with tearing of my hair,
Till they reduce the wrongs done to my father.
BARABAS
No, Abigail, things past recovery
Are hardly cured with exclamations.
Be silent, daughter, sufferance breeds ease,   240
And time may yield us an occasion
Which on the sudden cannot serve the turn.
Besides, my girl, think me not all so fond
As negligently to forgo so much
Without provision for thyself and me.   245
Ten thousand portagues, besides great pearls,
Rich costly jewels, and stones infinite,
Fearing the worst of this before it fell,
I closely hid.
ABIGAIL   Where father?
BARABAS   In my house my girl.
ABIGAIL
Then shall they ne'er be seen of Barabas: 250
For they have seized upon thy house and wares.
BARABAS
But they will give me leave once more, I trow,
To go into my house.
ABIGAIL   That may they not:
For there I left the Governor placing nuns,
Displacing me; and of thy house they mean   255
To make a nunnery, where none but their own sect
Must enter in; men generally barred.
BARABAS
My gold, my gold, and all my wealth is gone.
You partial heavens, have I deserved this plague?
What will you thus oppose me, luckless stars,   260
To make me desperate in my poverty?
And knowing me impatient in distress

---

236 *rent* rend, tear
238–9 *things past … exclamations* proverbial (Tilley, C 921)
240 *sufferance … ease* proverbial (Tilley, S 955)
241–2 *And time … turn* time may eventually present us with a better opportunity
　　　than now it offers
243 *fond* foolish
246 *portagues* Portuguese gold coins
252 *trow* trust
256 *sect* sex, but perhaps resonant with the many references to sectarian division
　　　according to religion
260 *luckless* malignant

Think me so mad as I will hang myself,
That I may vanish o'er the earth in air,
And leave no memory that e'er I was?   265
No, I will live; nor loathe I this my life:
And since you leave me in the ocean thus
To sink or swim, and put me to my shifts,
I'll rouse my senses, and awake myself.
Daughter, I have it: thou perceiv'st the plight   270
Wherein these Christians have oppressèd me:
Be ruled by me, for in extremity
We ought to make bar of no policy.

ABIGAIL

Father, whate'er it be to injure them
That have so manifestly wrongèd us,   275
What will not Abigail attempt?

BARABAS   Why so;
Then thus, thou told'st me they have turned my house
Into a nunnery, and some nuns are there.

ABIGAIL

I did.

BARABAS Then Abigail, there must my girl
Entreat the abbess to be entertained.   280

ABIGAIL

How, as a nun?

BARABAS   Ay, daughter, for religion
Hides many mischiefs from suspicion.

ABIGAIL

Ay, but father they will suspect me there.

BARABAS

Let 'em suspect, but be thou so precise
As they may think it done of holiness.   285
Entreat 'em fair, and give them friendly speech,
And seem to them as if thy sins were great,
Till thou hast gotten to be entertained.

---

268 *put me ... shifts* force me to fend for myself. Both this and 'sink or swim' are
   proverbial (Tilley, S 485; S 337).
273 *make bar ... policy* rule out no strategy
276–7 ed. (Q Why ... house / Into ...)
280 *entertained* received, admitted as a nun
281–2 *religion ... suspicion* Compare the relevant portions of Machiavelli's *Prince*
   concerning the political uses of religion (esp. chapter XVIII) with the statements
   of Machevill in the Prologue and with Gentillet's attacks on the 'atheism' of
   Machiavellians; cf. Minshull's analysis.
284 *precise* scrupulous; often pejoratively applied to Puritans
286 *Entreat 'em fair* present yourself ingratiatingly

ABIGAIL
  Thus father shall I much dissemble.
BARABAS   Tush,
  As good dissemble that thou never mean'st   290
  As first mean truth and then dissemble it;
  A counterfeit profession is better
  Than unseen hypocrisy.
ABIGAIL
  Well father, say I be entertained,
  What then shall follow?
BARABAS   This shall follow then;   295
  There have I hid close underneath the plank
  That runs along the upper chamber floor,
  The gold and jewels which I kept for thee.
  But here they come; be cunning Abigail.
ABIGAIL
  Then father go with me.
BARABAS   No, Abigail, in this   300
  It is not necessary I be seen.
  For I will seem offended with thee for't.
  Be close, my girl, for this must fetch my gold.

Enter three FRIARS [JACOMO *and* BERNARDINE *among
them] and two* NUNS [*one the* ABBESS]

JACOMO
  Sisters, we now are almost at the new-made nunnery.
1 NUN
  The better; for we love not to be seen: 305
  'Tis thirty winters long since some of us
  Did stray so far amongst the multitude.
JACOMO
  But, madam, this house
  And waters of this new-made nunnery
  Will much delight you.   310
1 NUN
  It may be so: but who comes here?

289–90 ed. (Q Thus ... dissemble. / Tush ... mean'st)
290–1 *As good ... dissemble it* It's no worse to deceive deliberately than to begin with
    true intentions and subsequently turn to hypocrisy
292–3 *A counterfeit profession ... unseen hypocrisy* This passage seems to say that self-
    conscious religious hypocrisy is preferable to an unwitting ideological blindness;
    see Hodge.
294 *say* suppose
301 It is necessary I should not be seen
304 *JACOMO* ed. (Q *1 Fry.*)

ABIGAIL

Grave Abbess, and you happy virgins' guide,
Pity the state of a distressèd maid.

ABBESS

What art thou daughter?

ABIGAIL

The hopeless daughter of a hapless Jew,   315
The Jew of Malta, wretched Barabas;
Sometimes the owner of a goodly house,
Which they have now turned to a nunnery.

ABBESS

Well, daughter, say, what is thy suit with us?

ABIGAIL

Fearing the afflictions which my father feels   320
Proceed from sin, or want of faith in us,
I'd pass away my life in penitence,
And be a novice in your nunnery,
To make atonement for my labouring soul.

JACOMO

No doubt, brother, but this proceedeth of the spirit.   325

BERNARDINE

Ay, and of a moving spirit too, brother; but come,
Let us entreat she may be entertained.

ABBESS

Well, daughter, we admit you for a nun.

ABIGAIL

First let me as a novice learn to frame
My solitary life to your strait laws,   330
And let me lodge where I was wont to lie;
I do not doubt by your divine precepts
And mine own industry, but to profit much.

BARABAS

(As much I hope as all I hid is worth.)

312 *you happy virgins' guide* This portion of the line may be addressed to the friar.
315 Cf. Hieronimo's line from *The Spanish Tragedy*: 'The hopeless father of a hapless son' (IV.iv.84).
317 *Sometimes* sometime, formerly
320 *feels* ed. (Q *feels,*)
324 *labouring* struggling, troubled
325 *proceedeth of the spirit* comes of the Holy Spirit
326 BERNARDINE ed. (Q *2 Fry.*)
    moving This and subsequent lines (see III.vi) permit interpretation in a sexual sense.
330 *strait* strict, confining
334 ed. (Q has a marginal '*aside*')

ABBESS
  Come daughter, follow us.   335
BARABAS
  Why how now Abigail, what mak'st thou
  Amongst these hateful Christians?
JACOMO
  Hinder her not, thou man of little faith,
  For she has mortified herself.
BARABAS   How, mortified!
JACOMO
  And is admitted to the sisterhood.   340
BARABAS
  Child of perdition, and thy father's shame,
  What wilt thou do among these hateful fiends?
  I charge thee on my blessing that thou leave
  These devils, and their damnèd heresy.
ABIGAIL
  Father give me –
BARABAS   Nay back, Abigail   345
  (And think upon the jewels and the gold,
  The board is markèd thus that covers it).

         [*Makes sign of the cross*]

  Away, accursèd from thy father's sight.
JACOMO
  Barabas, although thou art in misbelief,
  And wilt not see thine own afflictions,   350
  Yet let thy daughter be no longer blind.
BARABAS
  Blind, friar? I reck not thy persuasions.

336 *what mak'st thou* what are you doing?
338 *thou man of little faith* biblical phrasing (e.g. Matthew 6.30, 8.26)
339 *has mortified herself* has died to worldly values
343 *charge* command
345–8 *Nay back ... sight* Abigail apparently moves toward Barabas, allowing him to whisper to her between his two expressions of repulse. Q prints '*Whispers to her*' opposite line 346.
347 *thus* A standard Elizabethan indication of stage business; the text prints a cross-like dagger at 'thus' in line 353.
350 *wilt not see* The Friar attributes Barabas's Jewish faith to his wilfully obstinate spiritual blindness.
352 *Blind, friar?* ed. (Q Blind, Fryer,)
  reck not pay no heed to

(The board is markèd thus † that covers it.)
For I had rather die, than see her thus.
Wilt thou forsake me too in my distress,   355
Seducèd daughter? (Go forget not.)
Becomes it Jews to be so credulous?
(Tomorrow early I'll be at the door.)
No come not at me, if thou wilt be damned,
Forget me, see me not, and so be gone.   360
(Farewell. Remember tomorrow morning.)
Out, out thou wretch.

[*Exeunt*: BARABAS *on one side*; FRIARS, ABBESS,
NUN, *and* ABIGAIL *on the other*]

Enter MATHIAS

MATHIAS
Who's this? Fair Abigail the rich Jew's daughter
Become a nun? Her father's sudden fall
Has humbled her and brought her down to this: 365
Tut, she were fitter for a tale of love
Than to be tirèd out with orisons:
And better would she far become a bed
Embracèd in a friendly lover's arms,
Than rise at midnight to a solemn mass.   370

Enter LODOWICK

LODOWICK
Why how now Don Mathias, in a dump?
MATHIAS
Believe me, noble Lodowick, I have seen
The strangest sight, in my opinion,
That ever I beheld.
LODOWICK   What was't, I prithee?
MATHIAS
A fair young maid scarce fourteen years of age,   375
The sweetest flower in Cytherea's field,
Cropped from the pleasures of the fruitful earth,

353–61 Q prints lines 353, 358, 361 and portions of line 356 in italics. Next to lines
     356 and 358 '*aside to her*' appears in the margin.
356 *Seducèd daughter?* ed. (Q Seduced Daughter,)
357 *credulous?* ed. (Q credulous,)
364 *Become a nun? Her* ed. (Q Become a Nun, her)
367 *orisons* prayers
371 *in a dump* in a state of gloom
374 *was't, I* ed. (Q wast I)
376 *Cytherea* Venus

And strangely metamorphosed nun.
LODOWICK
  But say, what was she?
MATHIAS   Why the rich Jew's daughter.
LODOWICK
  What Barabas, whose goods were lately seized?   380
  Is she so fair?
MATHIAS   And matchless beautiful;
  As had you seen her 'twould have moved your heart,
  Though countermured with walls of brass, to love,
  Or at the least to pity.
LODOWICK
  And if she be so fair as you report,   385
  'Twere time well spent to go and visit her:
  How say you, shall we?
MATHIAS
  I must and will, sir, there's no remedy.
LODOWICK
  And so will I too, or it shall go hard.
  Farewell Mathias.
MATHIAS   Farewell Lodowick.   390

                                              Exeunt

Act II [Scene i]

Enter BARABAS *with a light*

BARABAS
  Thus like the sad presaging raven that tolls
  The sick man's passport in her hollow beak,
  And in the shadow of the silent night
  Doth shake contagion from her sable wings,
  Vexed and tormented runs poor Barabas   5
  With fatal curses towards these Christians.
  The incertain pleasures of swift-footed time
  Have ta'en their flight, and left me in despair;

---

378 *metamorphosed nun* transformed to a nun. Many editions add to this line to make
    it read: 'And strangely metamorphosed to a nun'.

383 *countermured* ed. (Q countermin'd) fortified with a double wall

385 *And if* if

389 *or it shall go hard* come what may

  1 *presaging ... tolls* foreboding ... announces

  2 *passport* i.e. allowing entry to death's kingdom

  4 *wings,* ed. (Q wings;)

And of my former riches rests no more
But bare remembrance; like a soldier's scar,   10
That has no further comfort for his maim.
Oh thou that with a fiery pillar led'st
The sons of Israel through the dismal shades,
Light Abraham's offspring; and direct the hand
Of Abigail this night; or let the day   15
Turn to eternal darkness after this:
No sleep can fasten on my watchful eyes,
Nor quiet enter my distempered thoughts,
Till I have answer of my Abigail.

Enter ABIGAIL *above*

ABIGAIL
Now have I happily espied a time   20
To search the plank my father did appoint;
And here behold, unseen, where I have found
The gold, the pearls, and jewels which he hid.
BARABAS
Now I remember those old women's words,
Who in my wealth would tell me winter's tales,   25
And speak of spirits and ghosts that glide by night
About the place where treasure hath been hid:
And now methinks that I am one of those:
For whilst I live, here lives my soul's sole hope,
And when I die, here shall my spirit walk.   30
ABIGAIL
Now that my father's fortune were so good
As but to be about this happy place;
'Tis not so happy: yet when we parted last,
He said he would attend me in the morn.
Then, gentle sleep, where'er his body rests,   35
Give charge to Morpheus that he may dream

---

9 *rests* remains

11 *maim* wound

12–13 See Exodus 13.21–2.

18 *distempered* agitated

20–2 *Now ... here, behold, unseen,* ed. (Q (unseen)) Abigail, like her father in being
unaware that anyone else is on-stage, is represented as discovering the treasure
as she speaks.
appoint designate

25 *wealth* time of prosperity
winter's tales fanciful stories

31 *Now that* Now if only

36 *Morpheus* son of sleep and god of dreams (cf. Ovid, *Metamorphoses* XI.623ff)

A golden dream, and of the sudden walk,
Come and receive the treasure I have found.
BARABAS
Bien para todos mi ganada no es:
As good go on, as sit so sadly thus.   40
But stay, what star shines yonder in the east?
The loadstar of my life, if Abigail.
Who's there?
ABIGAIL   Who's that?
BARABAS   Peace, Abigail, 'tis I.
ABIGAIL
Then father here receive thy happiness.
BARABAS
Hast thou't?   [ABIGAIL] *Throws down bags*   45
ABIGAIL
Here,
Hast thou't?
There's more, and more, and more.
BARABAS   Oh my girl,
My gold, my fortune, my felicity;
Strength to my soul, death to mine enemy;   50
Welcome the first beginner of my bliss:
Oh Abigail, Abigail, that I had thee here too,
Then my desires were fully satisfied.
But I will practise thy enlargement thence:
Oh girl, oh gold, oh beauty, oh my bliss! *Hugs his bags* 55
ABIGAIL
Father, it draweth towards midnight now,
And 'bout this time the nuns begin to wake;
To shun suspicion, therefore, let us part.
BARABAS
Farewell my joy, and by my fingers take
A kiss from him that sends it from his soul.   60
Now Phoebus ope the eye-lids of the day,
And for the raven wake the morning lark,
That I may hover with her in the air,

37 *walk* often amended to 'wake,' but possibly meaning 'arise' or 'sleepwalk'
39 *Bien para todos mi ganada no es:* ed. (Q *Birn para todos, my ganada no er:*) (Spanish)
My gain is not good for everybody
42 *loadstar* guiding star
46–8 *Here ... more, and more, and more* The short lines and repetitions may suggest
repeated action of throwing down the bags.
54 *practise thy enlargement* contrive your release
61 *Phoebus* Apollo, god of light and the sun
62 *for* in place of

Singing o'er these, as she does o'er her young.
Hermoso placer de los dineros.   65

Exeunt

[Act II, Scene ii]

Enter GOVERNOR [FERNEZE], MARTIN DEL BOSCO, *the* KNIGHTS
[*and* OFFICERS]

FERNEZE
Now Captain tell us whither thou art bound?
Whence is thy ship that anchors in our road?
And why thou cam'st ashore without our leave?
BOSCO
Governor of Malta, hither am I bound;
My ship, the Flying Dragon, is of Spain,   5
And so am I, Del Bosco is my name;
Vice-admiral unto the Catholic king.
1 KNIGHT
'Tis true, my lord, therefore entreat him well.
BOSCO
Our fraught is Grecians, Turks, and Afric Moors,
For late upon the coast of Corsica,   10
Because we vailed not to the Turkish fleet,
Their creeping galleys had us in the chase:
But suddenly the wind began to rise,
And then we luffed and tacked, and fought at ease:
Some have we fired, and many have we sunk;   15
But one amongst the rest became our prize:
The captain's slaine, the rest remain our slaves,
Of whom we would make sale in Malta here.
FERNEZE
Martin del Bosco, I have heard of thee;
Welcome to Malta, and to all of us;   20
But to admit a sale of these thy Turks

---

65 *Hermoso placer de los dineros* ed. (Q *Hermoso piarer, de les Denirch*) (Spanish)
   beautiful pleasure of money

0.1 FERNEZE Q calls Ferneze 'Governor' throughout the scene.

7 *Catholic king* according to Bawcutt a traditional title of the king of Spain

9 *fraught* cargo

11 *vailed* lowered sails in token of respect
   Turkish ed. (Q Spanish)

14 *luffed and tacked* ed. (Q left, and tooke) turned our ship into the wind and sailed
   obliquely against it

15 *fired* burned

We may not, nay we dare not give consent
By reason of a tributary league.

1 KNIGHT

Del Bosco, as thou lovest and honour'st us,
Persuade our Governor against the Turk;   25
This truce we have is but in hope of gold,
And with that sum he craves might we wage war.

BOSCO

Will Knights of Malta be in league with Turks,
And buy it basely too for sums of gold?
My lord, remember that to Europe's shame,   · 30
The Christian isle of Rhodes, from whence you came,
Was lately lost, and you were stated here
To be at deadly enmity with Turks.

FERNEZE

Captain we know it, but our force is small.

BOSCO

What is the sum that Calymath requires?   35

FERNEZE

A hundred thousand crowns.

BOSCO

My lord and king hath title to this isle,
And he means quickly to expel them hence;
Therefore be ruled by me, and keep the gold:
I'll write unto his Majesty for aid,   40
And not depart until I see you free.

FERNEZE

On this condition shall thy Turks be sold.
Go officers and set them straight in show.

                   [*Exeunt* OFFICERS]

Bosco, thou shalt be Malta's general;
We and our warlike knights will follow thee   45
Against these barbarous misbelieving Turks.

---

23 *tributary league* an alliance involving monetary payment

27 *he* the Turk

32 *lately lost* Rhodes fell to the Turks in 1522; in 1530 Malta was granted to the Knights by Charles V.
    stated installed in office

38 *them* ed. (Q you) Editors have assumed a confusion of pronouns here like the confusion of enemies in line 11; however, as Bawcutt argues, it is possible that the uncertainty is authorial. A multiple and evolving sense of who is the enemy of whom would fit with Emily Bartels's account of the play in terms of imperialism ('Malta, the Jew, and the Fictions of Difference: Colonialist Discourse in Marlowe's *Jew of Malta*', *ELR* 20 (1990), 3–16).

46 *misbelieving* non-Christian

BOSCO
  So shall you imitate those you succeed:
  For when their hideous force environed Rhodes,
  Small though the number was that kept the town,
  They fought it out, and not a man survived   50
  To bring the hapless news to Christendom.
FERNEZE
  So will we fight it out; come let's away:
  Proud-daring Calymath, instead of gold,
  We'll send thee bullets wrapped in smoke and fire:
  Claim tribute where thou wilt, we are resolved,   55
  Honour is bought with blood and not with gold.

Exeunt

[Act II, Scene iii]

Enter OFFICERS *with* [ITHAMORE *and other*] SLAVES

1 OFFICER
  This is the market-place, here let 'em stand:
  Fear not their sale, for they'll be quickly bought.
2 OFFICER
  Every one's price is written on his back,
  And so much must they yield or not be sold.

Enter BARABAS

1 OFFICER
  Here comes the Jew, had not his goods been seized,   5
  He'd give us present money for them all.
BARABAS
  In spite of these swine-eating Christians,
  Unchosen nation, never circumcised;
  Such as, poor villains, were ne'er thought upon
  Till Titus and Vespasian conquered us,   10

47–51 *So ... Christendom* The siege of Rhodes in 1522 did not result in the total
    destruction Del Bosco claims.
51 *hapless* unfortunate
54 *send thee* ed. (Q send the)
  4 s.d. Q has entry directions for Barabas here and at line 7.
  6 *present money* ready cash
8–10 ed. (Q (Vnchosen ... circumciz'd; / Such ... vpon / Till ... vs.))
  9 *such as, poor villains,* ed. (Q such as poore villaines)
    villains low fellows
    ne'er thought upon disregarded
10 *Titus and Vespasian* Vespasian and his son Titus, successive Roman Emperors,
    led the campaigns that resulted in the fall of Jerusalem in A.D. 70.

Am I become as wealthy as I was:
They hoped my daughter would ha' been a nun;
But she's at home, and I have bought a house
As great and fair as is the Governor's;
And there in spite of Malta will I dwell: 15
Having Ferneze's hand, whose heart I'll have;
Ay, and his son's too, or it shall go hard.
I am not of the tribe of Levi, I,
That can so soon forget an injury.
We Jews can fawn like spaniels when we please;   20
And when we grin we bite, yet are our looks
As innocent and harmless as a lamb's.
I learned in Florence how to kiss my hand,
Heave up my shoulders when they call me dog,
And duck as low as any bare-foot friar,   25
Hoping to see them starve upon a stall,
Or else be gathered for in our synagogue;
That when the offering-basin comes to me,
Even for charity I may spit into't.
Here comes Don Lodowick the Governor's son,   30
One that I love for his good father's sake.

Enter LODOWICK

LODOWICK
I hear the wealthy Jew walked this way;
I'll seek him out, and so insinuate,
That I may have a sight of Abigail;
For Don Mathias tells me she is fair.   35
BARABAS
(Now will I show myself to have more of the serpent than
   the dove; that is, more knave than fool.)
LODOWICK
Yond walks the Jew, now for fair Abigail.

---

16 *Ferneze's hand* either Ferneze's written assurance of safety or his handshake in
   friendship
18 *tribe of Levi* the tribe associated with priestliness and jurisdiction over the cities
   of refuge (Joshua 20–1)
25 *duck* bow humbly (see III.iii.53)
26 *stall* a commercial display platform sometimes used for a bed by impoverished
   vagrants
27 *be gathered for* have a collection taken for them
33 *insinuate* work myself into favour
36–7 ed. (Q Now ... serpent / Then ... foole.)
36 *more of the serpent than the dove* more cunning than innocence (twisting the
   admonition of Matthew 10.16: 'be ye therefore wise as serpentes, and innocent
   as doues')

BARABAS

(Ay, ay, no doubt but she's at your command.)

LODOWICK

Barabas, thou know'st I am the Governor's son.   40

BARABAS

I would you were his father too, sir, that's all the harm
I wish you. (The slave looks like a hog's cheek new
singed.)

[BARABAS *turns away*]

LODOWICK

Whither walk'st thou Barabas?

BARABAS

No further: 'tis a custom held with us,   45
That when we speak with Gentiles like to you,
We turn into the air to purge ourselves:
For unto us the promise doth belong.

LODOWICK

Well, Barabas, canst help me to a diamond?

BARABAS

Oh, sir, your father had my diamonds.   50
Yet I have one left that will serve your turn:
I mean my daughter. (But ere he shall have her
I'll sacrifice her on a pile of wood.
I ha' the poison of the city for him,
And the white leprosy.)   55

LODOWICK

What sparkle does it give without a foil?

BARABAS

The diamond that I talk of, ne'er was foiled
(But when he touches it, it will be foiled).
Lord Lodowick, it sparkles bright and fair.

41–3 ed. (Q I ... harm / I wish you: the slave ... sindg'd.)
    hog's cheek new singed i.e. Lodowick is recently shaven
48 *the promise* See I.i.104–5n.
52 ed. (Q I mean my daughter: – but ...) Q prints '*aside*' opposite line 53, but the
    dash in the Q version of line 52 may indicate the beginning of the aside (as
    apparently in lines 61 and 68). However, as Craik points out, 'I mean my
    daughter' may be an aside, since Lodowick and Barabas 'continue talking of
    Abigail obliquely as a diamond'.
54–5 ed. (Q the / White)
    poison of the city ... white leprosy not satisfactorily explained but apparently
    references to a virulent poison and a natural disease associated with cities, such
    as the plague
56 *foil* thin metallic leaf set under a gem to add to its brilliance
57 *foiled* set by a jeweller
58 ed. (Q But ... foiled:)
    foiled defiled, dishonoured

LODOWICK

Is it square or pointed? Pray let me know.   60

BARABAS

Pointed it is, good sir (but not for you).

LODOWICK

I like it much the better.

BARABAS   So do I too.

LODOWICK

How shows it by night?

BARABAS   Outshines Cynthia's rays:

You'll like it better far a' nights than days.

LODOWICK

And what's the price?   65

BARABAS

(Your life and if you have it.) O my lord

We will not jar about the price; come to my house

And I will give't your honour (with a vengeance).

LODOWICK

No, Barabas, I will deserve it first.

BARABAS

Good sir,   70

Your father has deserved it at my hands,

Who of mere charity and Christian ruth,

To bring me to religious purity,

And as it were in catechizing sort,

To make me mindful of my mortal sins,   75

Against my will, and whether I would or no,

Seized all I had, and thrust me out-a-doors,

And made my house a place for nuns most chaste.

LODOWICK

No doubt your soul shall reap the fruit of it.

60 ed. (Q pointed,)

60–1 *pointed* denoting the cut of a gem, but used by Barabas to mean 'appointed' or 'promised'

61 ed. (Q Pointed it is, good Sir, – but not for you.) Q has an '*aside*' in the margin.

63 *Cynthia* the moon

64 Q marks the line '*aside*'; Craik suggests this may refer to line 66.

66 ed. (Q Your life and if you haue it. – Oh my Lord)
    and if if

67 *jar* quarrel

68 ed. (Q And I will giu't your honour – with a vengeance.) Line 68 is marked '*aside*' in Q.

70–1 ed. (Q *one line*)

72 *ruth* pity

74 *in catechizing sort* in the manner of religious instruction

BARABAS

Ay, but my lord, the harvest is far off: 80
And yet I know the prayers of those nuns
And holy friars, having money for their pains,
Are wondrous; (and indeed do no man good)
And seeing they are not idle, but still doing,
'Tis likely they in time may reap some fruit,   85
I mean in fullness of perfection.

LODOWICK

Good Barabas glance not at our holy nuns.

BARABAS

No, but I do it through a burning zeal
(Hoping ere long to set the house afire;
For though they do awhile increase and multiply,   90
I'll have a saying to that nunnery).
As for the diamond, sir, I told you of,
Come home and there's no price shall make us part,
Even for your honourable father's sake.
(It shall go hard but I will see your death.)   95
But now I must be gone to buy a slave.

LODOWICK

And, Barabas, I'll bear thee company.

BARABAS

Come then, here's the marketplace; what's the price of
this slave, two hundred crowns? Do the Turks weigh so
much?   100

1 OFFICER

Sir, that's his price.

BARABAS

What, can he steal that you demand so much?
Belike he has some new trick for a purse;

---

83 ed. (Q Are wondrous; *and indeed doe no man good*:) This line is also marked with
a marginal '*aside*'. Line 87 suggests that Lodowick hears the remainder of
Barabas's speech.

84–6 *still doing* always copulating
   still doing ... perfection Barabas employs the terms of Lodowick's theological
   discourse to suggest the hypocrisy of the nuns' and friars' claims to chastity.

87 *glance not* do not criticize by innuendo

89–91 italicized in Q with marginal '*aside*' opposite line 90
   increase and multiply The nuns, while professing chastity, fulfil God's command
   to Noah (Genesis 9).
   have a saying to have something to say about

95 italicized in Q with marginal '*aside*'
   It shall go hard but unless prevented by the power of circumstances it will happen
   that

98–100 ed. (Q Come ... price / Of ... much?)

99 *Turks* ed. (Q *Turke*)

And if he has, he is worth three hundred plates,
So that, being bought, the town seal might be got	105
To keep him for his lifetime from the gallows.
The sessions day is critical to thieves,
And few or none 'scape but by being purged.

LODOWICK
Ratest thou this Moor but at two hundred plates?

1 OFFICER
No more, my lord.	110

BARABAS
Why should this Turk be dearer than that Moor?

1 OFFICER
Because he is young and has more qualities.

BARABAS
What, hast the philosopher's stone? And thou hast, break
my head with it, I'll forgive thee.

SLAVE
No sir, I can cut and shave.	115

BARABAS
Let me see, sirrah, are you not an old shaver?

SLAVE
Alas, sir, I am a very youth.

BARABAS
A youth? I'll buy you, and marry you to Lady Vanity if
you do well.

SLAVE
I will serve you, sir.	120

BARABAS
Some wicked trick or other. It may be under colour of
shaving, thou'lt cut my throat for my goods. Tell me,
hast thou thy health well?

104 *plates,* ed. (Q plats.) silver coins
104–8 *And if ... purged* he might be worth so much as a thief if one could get
    governmental assurance of pardon; trial days are fatal to thieves, few escaping
    the 'cure' of being hanged
112 *qualities* abilities
113–14 ed. (Q What ... hast, / Breake ... thee.)
113 *philosopher's stone* the much sought-after goal of alchemy, a stone that would turn
    other metals to gold
115–24 *Slave* ed. (Q *Itha.* or *Ith.*)
116 *old shaver* rogue, rascal
118–19 ed. (Q A ... vanity / If ... well.) *Youth* and *Vanity* are stock figures of the
    morality plays; as Craik observes, Barabas's promise to marry Youth to Vanity
    would encourage vice rather than virtue.
121–3 ed. (Q Some ... colour / Of ... goods. / Tell ... well?)
121 *colour* pretence

SLAVE
  Ay, passing well.
BARABAS
  So much the worse; I must have one that's sickly, and't   125
  be but for sparing vittles: 'tis not a stone of beef a day
  will maintain you in these chops; let me see one that's
  somewhat leaner.
1 OFFICER
  Here's a leaner, how like you him?
BARABAS
  Where wast thou born?   130
ITHAMORE
  In Thrace; brought up in Arabia.
BARABAS
  So much the better, thou art for my turn;
  An hundred crowns, I'll have him; there's the coin.
                                          [Pays money]
1 OFFICER
  Then mark him, sir, and take him hence.
BARABAS
  (Ay, mark him, you were best, for this is he   135
  That by my help shall do much villainy.)
  My lord farewell: [to ITHAMORE] come sirrah you are
      mine.
  [To LODOWICK] As for the diamond, it shall be yours;
  I pray, sir, be no stranger at my house,
  All that I have shall be at your command.   140

          Enter MATHIAS [and his] MOTHER [KATHERINE]

MATHIAS
  (What makes the Jew and Lodowick so private?
  I fear me 'tis about fair Abigail.)
BARABAS
  Yonder comes Don Mathias, let us stay;

125–8 ed. (Q So ... sickly, / And ... day / Will ... one / That's ... leaner.)
125–6 *and't be but for* ed. (Q And be but for) if only for the sake of
126 *stone* fourteen pounds
127 *chops* jowls
130 *wast* ed. (Q was)
131 *Thrace* ed. (Q Trace)
132 *for my turn;* ed. (Q for my turn,) suited for my purposes
135 *mark* observe, pay attention to
141 s.d. ed. (Q *Enter Mathias, Mater*; her speeches so headed throughout)
143 *let us stay* let us break off our talk

He loves my daughter, and she holds him dear:
But I have sworn to frustrate both their hopes,   145
And be revenged upon the – (Governor).

[Exit LODOWICK]

KATHERINE
This Moor is comeliest, is he not? Speak, son.
MATHIAS
No, this is the better, mother, view this well.
BARABAS
(Seem not to know me here before your mother,
Lest she mistrust the match that is in hand: 150
When you have brought her home, come to my house;
Think of me as thy father; son farewell.
MATHIAS
But wherefore talked Don Lodowick with you?
BARABAS
Tush man, we talked of diamonds, not of Abigail.)
KATHERINE
Tell me, Mathias, is not that the Jew?   155
BARABAS
As for the comment on the Maccabees,
I have it, sir, and 'tis at your command.
MATHIAS
Yes, madam, and my talk with him was
About the borrowing of a book or two.
KATHERINE
Converse not with him, he is cast off from heaven.   160
[*To* OFFICER] Thou hast thy crowns, fellow, [*to* MATHIAS]
    come let's away.
MATHIAS
Sirrah, Jew, remember the book.
BARABAS
Marry will I, sir.

Exeunt [MATHIAS *and* MOTHER *with* SLAVE]

144–6 The addressee of these lines is difficult to determine. Q's punctuation of line
    146 (And be reveng'd upon the — Governor.) is typical of its treatment of
    Barabas's asides at the end of lines, and this suggests that he addresses most of
    the speech to Lodowick; but, as Bawcutt points out, at line 287 Lodowick appears
    unaware of Abigail's love for Mathias, so perhaps he exits as Mathias enters.
150 *mistrust* suspect
156 *comment on the Maccabees* commentary on the two apocryphal biblical books of
    the Maccabees
163 s.d. (Q places after line 161)

1 OFFICER
    Come, I have made a reasonable market, let's away.
                    [*Exeunt* OFFICERS *with* SLAVES]

BARABAS
    Now let me know thy name, and therewithal   165
    Thy birth, condition, and profession.

ITHAMORE
    Faith, sir, my birth is but mean, my name's Ithamore,
    my profession what you please.

BARABAS
    Hast thou no trade? Then listen to my words,
    And I will teach that shall stick by thee: 170
    First be thou void of these affections,
    Compassion, love, vain hope, and heartless fear,
    Be moved at nothing, see thou pity none,
    But to thyself smile when the Christians moan.

ITHAMORE
    Oh brave, master, I worship your nose for this.   175

BARABAS
    As for myself, I walk abroad a-nights
    And kill sick people groaning under walls:
    Sometimes I go about and poison wells;
    And now and then, to cherish Christian thieves,
    I am content to lose some of my crowns;   180
    That I may, walking in my gallery,
    See 'em go pinioned along by my door.
    Being young I studied physic, and began
    To practise first upon the Italian;
    There I enriched the priests with burials,   185
    And always kept the sexton's arms in ure
    With digging graves and ringing dead men's knells:
    And after that was I an engineer,

166 *condition* social standing
167 *mean* low
170 *stick by thee* be worth remembering
171 *affections* feelings
172 *heartless* cowardly
175 *brave* wonderful
    your nose alluding to Barabas's huge nose (see III.iii.10)
181 *gallery* balcony (see V.v.33)
182 *pinioned* with arms tied together
183 *physic* medicine
186 *ure* use
188 *engineer* builder of military engines

And in the wars 'twixt France and Germany,
Under pretence of helping Charles the Fifth,   190
Slew friend and enemy with my stratagems.
Then after that was I an usurer,
And with extorting, cozening, forfeiting,
And tricks belonging unto brokery,
I filled the jails with bankrouts in a year,   195
And with young orphans planted hospitals,
And every moon made some or other mad,
And now and then one hang himself for grief,
Pinning upon his breast a long great scroll
How I with interest tormented him.   200
But mark how I am blest for plaguing them,
I have as much coin as will buy the town.
But tell me now, how hast thou spent thy time?
ITHAMORE
Faith, master,
In setting Christian villages on fire,   205
Chaining of eunuchs, binding galley-slaves.
One time I was an hostler in an inn,
And in the night time secretly would I steal
To travellers' chambers, and there cut their throats:
Once at Jerusalem, where the pilgrims kneeled,   210
I strowèd powder on the marble stones,
And therewithal their knees would rankle, so
That I have laughed a-good to see the cripples
Go limping home to Christendom on stilts.
BARABAS
Why this is something: make account of me   215
As of thy fellow; we are villains both:
Both circumcisèd, we hate Christians both:

189–90 Struggles between the forces of the Holy Roman Emperor, Charles V (1500–
          58), and the French King, Francis I, continued between 1519 and 1558.
192 *usurer* money-lender; usually associated with high rates (cf. IV.i.54)
193 *cozening* cheating
     forfeiting profiting from the failure of borrowers to repay their loans
194 *brokery* dishonest financial transactions
195 *bankrouts* bankrupts
196 *planted* furnished
     hospitals charitable institutions, almshouses
204–5 ed. (Q *one line*)
207 *hostler* stable keeper
212 *rankle* fester
213 *a-good* heartily
214 *stilts* crutches
215 *make account of me* think of me

Be true and secret, thou shalt want no gold.
But stand aside, here comes Don Lodowick.

Enter LODOWICK

LODOWICK
  Oh Barabas well met;   220
  Where is the diamond you told me of?
BARABAS
  I have it for you, sir; please you walk in with me:
  What, ho, Abigail; open the door I say.

Enter ABIGAIL

ABIGAIL
  In good time, father, here are letters come
  From Ormus, and the post stays here within.   225
BARABAS
  Give me the letters, daughter, do you hear?
  Entertain Lodowick the Governor's son
  With all the courtesy you can afford;
  Provided, that you keep your maidenhead.
  Use him as if he were a (Philistine.   230
  Dissemble, swear, protest, vow to love him,
  He is not of the seed of Abraham.)
  I am a little busy, sir, pray pardon me.
  Abigail, bid him welcome for my sake.
ABIGAIL
  For your sake and his own he's welcome hither.   235
BARABAS
  Daughter, a word more. (Kiss him, speak him fair,
  And like a cunning Jew so cast about,
  That ye be both made sure ere you come out.

220–1 ed. (Q Oh . . . Diamond / You . . . of?)

225 *Ormus* town on the Persian Gulf, known in the Renaissance for trading in
    luxuries
    post messenger

226–32 This edition follows Q, which has '*aside*' opposite line 230 and prints the
    word 'Philistine' and lines 231–2 in italics. As Craik points out, it is typical of
    Barabas to employ final words to reverse the sense of phrases; the advice to
    Abigail in line 229, as Bawcutt observes, may be a coarse joke intended for
    Lodowick's appreciation. Q's comma after 'Provided' may suggest a slightly
    retarded ponderous pace, potentially indicative of self-irony.

230 *Philistine* biblical enemies of the Jews

236 ed. (Q Daughter, a word more; kisse him, speake him faire,)

237 *cast about* devise

238 *made sure* betrothed

ABIGAIL

Oh father, Don Mathias is my love.

BARABAS

I know it: yet I say make love to him;   240
Do, it is requisite it should be so.)
Nay on my life it is my factor's hand,
But go you in, I'll think upon the account:

[Exeunt LODOWICK *and* ABIGAIL]

The account is made, for Lodowick dies.
My factor sends me word a merchant's fled   245
That owes me for a hundred tun of wine:
I weigh it thus much; I have wealth enough.
For now by this has he kissed Abigail;
And she vows love to him, and he to her.
As sure as heaven rained manna for the Jews,   250
So sure shall he and Don Mathias die:
His father was my chiefest enemy.

Enter MATHIAS

Whither goes Don Mathias? Stay a while.

MATHIAS

Whither but to my fair love Abigail?

BARABAS

Thou know'st, and heaven can witness it is true, 255
That I intend my daughter shall be thine.

MATHIAS

Ay, Barabas, or else thou wrong'st me much.

BARABAS

Oh heaven forbid I should have such a thought.
Pardon me though I weep; the Governor's son
Will, whether I will or no, have Abigail: 260
He sends her letters, bracelets, jewels, rings.

MATHIAS

Does she receive them?

BARABAS

She? No, Mathias, no, but sends them back,

---

242 *factor's hand* agent's handwriting
243 *account* financial reckoning, with a play on the next line's meaning of 'settling scores'
246 *tun* barrel
247 *thus much* Barabas probably makes a dismissive gesture.
248 *by this* by this time
250 *manna* food given the Jews by heaven (see Exodus 16)
252 *was* i.e. in the seizure of his property
252 s.d. follows 253 in Q

And when he comes, she locks herself up fast;
Yet through the keyhole will he talk to her,   265
While she runs to the window looking out
When you should come and hale him from the door.
MATHIAS
Oh treacherous Lodowick!
BARABAS
Even now as I came home, he slipped me in,
And I am sure he is with Abigail.   270
MATHIAS
I'll rouse him thence.   [*Draws a sword*]
BARABAS
Not for all Malta, therefore sheathe your sword;
If you love me, no quarrels in my house;
But steal you in, and seem to see him not;
I'll give him such a warning ere he goes   275
As he shall have small hopes of Abigail.
Away, for here they come.

Enter LODOWICK, ABIGAIL

MATHIAS
What hand in hand, I cannot suffer this.
BARABAS
Mathias, as thou lov'st me, not a word.
MATHIAS
Well, let it pass, another time shall serve.   *Exit* 280
LODOWICK
Barabas, is not that the widow's son?
BARABAS
Ay, and take heed, for he hath sworn your death.
LODOWICK
My death? What is the base-born peasant mad?
BARABAS
No, no, but happily he stands in fear
Of that which you, I think, ne'er dream upon,   285
My daughter here, a paltry silly girl.

264 *fast* securely
267 *hale* pull violently
269 *slipped me in* slipped in
271 *rouse* drive from concealment (as a hunter's quarry)
278 *suffer* endure
284 *happily* perhaps
284–6 Whatever the exact sense of these lines, it appears that Barabas means to elicit
    a declaration of love by insinuating that Mathias takes Abigail more seriously
    than does Lodowick.
286 *silly* unsophisticated

LODOWICK
  Why, loves she Don Mathias?
BARABAS
  Doth she not with her smiling answer you?
ABIGAIL
  (He has my heart, I smile against my will.)
LODOWICK
  Barabas, thou know'st I have loved thy daughter long.   290
BARABAS
  And so has she done you, even from a child.
LODOWICK
  And now I can no longer hold my mind.
BARABAS
  Nor I the affection that I bear to you.
LODOWICK
  This is thy diamond, tell me, shall I have it?
BARABAS
  Win it and wear it, it is yet unsoiled.   295
  Oh but I know your lordship would disdain
  To marry with the daughter of a Jew:
  And yet I'll give her many a golden cross
  With Christian posies round about the ring.
LODOWICK
  'Tis not thy wealth, but her that I esteem,   300
  Yet crave I thy consent.
BARABAS
  And mine you have, yet let me talk to her.
  (This offspring of Cain, this Jebusite
  That never tasted of the Passover,

---

287 *Why, loves* ed. (Q Why loves)
291 *even from a child* ever since childhood
292 *hold my mind* conceal my feelings
295 *unsoiled* undefiled, virginal
298 *cross* coin stamped with a cross
299 *Christian posies* pious mottoes to be found both on coins of the period and on wedding rings
302 ed. (Q And … her;)
302–15 *aside* opposite line 306 in Q
303 *offspring of Cain* a degenerate race in Jewish and Christian traditions, descended from the first biblical murderer
    Jebusite member of the original Canaanite tribe driven from Jerusalem by King David (see II Samuel 5)
304 *Passover* the important Jewish ritual, commemorating the deliverance from Egypt described in Exodus 12

Nor e'er shall see the land of Canaan,   305
Nor our Messias that is yet to come,
This gentle maggot Lodowick I mean,
Must be deluded: let him have thy hand,
But keep thy heart till Don Mathias comes.

ABIGAIL
What shall I be betrothed to Lodowick?   310

BARABAS
It's no sin to deceive a Christian;
For they themselves hold it a principle,
Faith is not to be held with heretics;
But all are heretics that are not Jews;
This follows well, and therefore daughter fear not.)   315
I have entreated her, and she will grant.

LODOWICK
Then gentle Abigail plight thy faith to me.

ABIGAIL
I cannot choose, seeing my father bids:
Nothing but death shall part my love and me.

LODOWICK
Now have I that for which my soul hath longed.   320

BARABAS
(So have not I, but yet I hope I shall.)

ABIGAIL
(Oh wretched Abigail, what hast thou done?)

LODOWICK
Why on the sudden is your colour changed?

ABIGAIL
I know not, but farewell, I must be gone.

---

305 *Canaan* the land promised the Jews in Genesis 17

306 *Messias* Messiah

307 *gentle maggot* punning on 'gentle' as 'gentleman', as 'gentile', and as a synonym for 'maggot'

311–13 This doctrine is a favourite object of Protestant polemic, which associated it with Catholic treachery as exemplified by the Council of Constance (1415) in its justification of action against Jan Hus despite an agreement of safe-conduct. See *2 Tamburlaine* II.i.

315 *This follows well* this is good logic

317 *plight thy faith* enter into a binding betrothal, promising to marry

318–19 Line 318 may be audible to Lodowick, since it could be understood to represent a traditional view of a daughter's obligation rather than mere constraint; Abigail equivocates in line 319, since 'my love' could be taken by Lodowick to refer to himself.

321 Q prints '*aside*' in the margin.

BARABAS

  Stay her, but let her not speak one word more.   325

LODOWICK

  Mute o' the sudden; here's a sudden change.

BARABAS

  Oh muse not at it, 'tis the Hebrews' guise,
  That maidens new betrothed should weep a while:
  Trouble her not, sweet Lodowick depart:
  She is thy wife, and thou shalt be mine heir.   330

LODOWICK

  Oh, is't the custom, then I am resolved;
  But rather let the brightsome heavens be dim,
  And nature's beauty choke with stifling clouds,
  Than my fair Abigail should frown on me.
  There comes the villain, now I'll be revenged.   335

Enter MATHIAS

BARABAS

  Be quiet Lodowick, it is enough
  That I have made thee sure to Abigail.

LODOWICK

  Well, let him go.   *Exit*

BARABAS

  Well, but for me, as you went in at doors
  You had been stabbed, but not a word on't now;   340
  Here must no speeches pass, nor swords be drawn.

MATHIAS

  Suffer me, Barabas, but to follow him.

BARABAS

  No; so shall I, if any hurt be done,
  Be made an accessary of your deeds;
  Revenge it on him when you meet him next.   345

MATHIAS

  For this I'll have his heart.

BARABAS

  Do so; lo here I give thee Abigail.

MATHIAS

  What greater gift can poor Mathias have?
  Shall Lodowick rob me of so fair a love?
  My life is not so dear as Abigail.   350

325 *stay her* either an injunction to Mathias to support Abigail in her distressed state
    or an aside to Ithamore commanding him to keep her quiet (see line 364)
327 *guise* customary manner
331 *resolved* satisfied
332 *rather* ed. (Q rathe)
342 *suffer* allow

BARABAS

My heart misgives me, that to cross your love,
He's with your mother, therefore after him.

MATHIAS

What, is he gone unto my mother?

BARABAS

Nay, if you will, stay till she comes herself.

MATHIAS

I cannot stay; for if my mother come,   355
She'll die with grief.   *Exit*

ABIGAIL

I cannot take my leave of him for tears:
Father, why have you thus incensed them both?

BARABAS

What's that to thee?

ABIGAIL   I'll make 'em friends again.

BARABAS

You'll make 'em friends?   360
Are there not Jews enow in Malta,
But thou must dote upon a Christian?

ABIGAIL

I will have Don Mathias, he is my love.

BARABAS

Yes, you shall have him: go put her in.

ITHAMORE

Ay, I'll put her in.   365

[*Puts* ABIGAIL *in*]

BARABAS

Now tell me, Ithamore, how lik'st thou this?

ITHAMORE

Faith master, I think by this
You purchase both their lives; is it not so?

BARABAS

True; and it shall be cunningly performed.

ITHAMORE

Oh, master, that I might have a hand in this.   370

351 *misgives me* makes me fear
    cross hinder, prevent
360–1 *You'll ... friends / Are* ed. (Q You'll ... Iewes / Enow)
    enow enough
364 *put her in* lock her up in the house
368 *purchase* obtain

BARABAS

Ay, so thou shalt, 'tis thou must do the deed:
Take this and bear it to Mathias straight,
And tell him that it comes from Lodowick.

ITHAMORE

'Tis poisoned, is it not?

BARABAS

No, no, and yet it might be done that way: 375
It is a challenge feigned from Lodowick.

ITHAMORE

Fear not, I'll so set this heart afire, that he shall verily
think it comes from him.

BARABAS

I cannot choose but like thy readiness:
Yet be not rash, but do it cunningly.   380

ITHAMORE

As I behave myself in this, employ me hereafter.

BARABAS

Away then.

Exit [ITHAMORE]

So, now will I go in to Lodowick,
And like a cunning spirit feign some lie,
Till I have set 'em both at enmity.   *Exit* 385

Act III [Scene i]

Enter [BELLAMIRA] *a* COURTESAN

BELLAMIRA

Since this town was besieged, my gain grows cold:
The time has been, that but for one bare night
A hundred ducats have been freely given:
But now against my will I must be chaste.
And yet I know my beauty doth not fail.   5
From Venice merchants, and from Padua

377–8 ed. (Q Feare . . . he / Shall . . . him.)

384 *spirit* devil

   0.s.d. *COURTESAN* high class prostitute

   1 *besieged* As Bennett notes, the siege does not truly begin until the defiance of the
      Turks in III.v. There may have been a rearrangement of scenes; or, as Bawcutt
      suggests, the mere presence of the Turkish fleet has effectively blockaded Malta.
      my . . . cold my profits have diminished

   2 *bare* single and/or naked

   6 *Padua / Were* ed. (Q Padua, / Were)
      Venice . . . Padua respectively, centres of trade and learning

Were wont to come rare-witted gentlemen,
Scholars I mean, learnèd and liberal;
And now, save Pilia-Borza, comes there none,
And he is very seldom from my house;   10
And here he comes.

Enter PILIA-BORZA

PILIA-BORZA
Hold thee, wench, there's something for thee to spend.

[*Offers bag of money*]

BELLAMIRA
'Tis silver, I disdain it.
PILIA-BORZA
Ay, but the Jew has gold,
And I will have it or it shall go hard.   15
BELLAMIRA
Tell me, how cam'st thou by this?
PILIA-BORZA
Faith, walking the back lanes through the gardens I
chanced to cast mine eye up to the Jew's counting-house,
where I saw some bags of money, and in the night I
clambered up with my hooks, and as I was taking my   20
choice, I heard a rumbling in the house; so I took only
this, and run my way: but here's the Jew's man.

Enter ITHAMORE

BELLAMIRA
Hide the bag.
PILIA-BORZA
Look not towards him, let's away: zoons what a looking
thou keep'st, thou'lt betray's anon.   25
                        [*Exeunt* BELLAMIRA *and* PILIA-BORZA]

---

8 *liberal* free spending (with double sense, like 'cold' and 'bare')
9 *Pilia-Borza* from the Italian for cutpurse or pickpocket
12 *Hold thee* here, take this
17–22 ed. Q Faith ... Gardens / I ... house / Where ... I / Clamber'd ... taking /
    My ... tooke / Onely ... man.)
18 *counting-house,* ed. (Q counting-house)
20 *hooks* standard item of burglary equipment
24–5 ed. (Q Looke ... away: / Zoon's ... keep'st, / Thou'lt ... anon.)
24 *zoons* zounds, a contraction of 'by God's wounds'
24–5 *looking ... keep'st* obvious staring you engage in
25 *anon* immediately

ITHAMORE
> O the sweetest face that ever I beheld! I know she is a
> courtesan by her attire: now would I give a hundred of
> the Jew's crowns that I had such a concubine.
> Well, I have delivered the challenge in such sort,
> As meet they will, and fighting die; brave sport.   *Exit*   30

[Act III, Scene ii]

Enter MATHIAS

MATHIAS
> This is the place, now Abigail shall see
> Whether Mathias holds her dear or no.

Enter LODOWICK *reading*

[LODOWICK]
> What, dares the villain write in such base terms?
[MATHIAS]
> I did it, and revenge it if thou dar'st.

Fight. Enter BARABAS *above*

BARABAS
> Oh bravely fought, and yet they thrust not home.   5
> Now Lodowick, now Mathias, so;   [*Both fall*]
> So now they have showed themselves to be tall fellows.
[VOICES] *within*
> Part 'em, part 'em.

26–8 ed. (Q O ... is / A ... hundred / Of ... Concubine.)

27 *attire* apparently a distinctive form of dress, whether the red taffeta worn by
some English prostitutes or the more elaborate gowns of their notorious Venetian
counterparts

29 *in such sort* in such a form

30 *brave sport* admirable jest

3–4 The text is doubtful. Q gives line 3 to Mathias and line 4 to Lodowick. The
entrance 'reading' and his use of the status terms 'villain' and 'base' argue that
it is Lodowick who reacts to a communication – probably Mathias's reply to
Barabas's forged challenge ('feigned from Lodowick' (II.iii.376)), since Mathias
here acknowledges 'I did it'; but later Ithamore claims to have also brought a
forged challenge to Lodowick (III.iii.19–21), so perhaps both Lodowick and
Mathias mistake a forgery for Mathias's own letter.

5 *home* deeply, mortally

6 *now ... now ... so* The lines suggest the sword strokes.

7 *tall* brave (ironically)

BARABAS
    Ay, part 'em now they are dead: farewell, farewell. *Exit*

        Enter GOVERNOR [FERNEZE], MOTHER [KATHERINE],
               [*with* CITIZENS]

FERNEZE
    What sight is this? My Lodowick slain!   10
    These arms of mine shall be thy sepulchre.
KATHERINE
    Who is this? My son Mathias slain!
FERNEZE
    Oh Lodowick! had'st thou perished by the Turk,
    Wretched Ferneze might have venged thy death.
KATHERINE
    Thy son slew mine, and I'll revenge his death.   15
FERNEZE
    Look, Katherine, look, thy son gave mine these wounds.
KATHERINE
    O leave to grieve me, I am grieved enough.
FERNEZE
    Oh that my sighs could turn to lively breath;
    And these my tears to blood, that he might live.
KATHERINE
    Who made them enemies?   20
FERNEZE
    I know not, and that grieves me most of all.
KATHERINE
    My son loved thine.
FERNEZE   And so did Lodowick him.
KATHERINE
    Lend me that weapon that did kill my son,
    And it shall murder me.
FERNEZE
    Nay Madam stay, that weapon was my son's,   25
    And on that rather should Ferneze die.
KATHERINE
    Hold, let's enquire the causers of their deaths,
    That we may venge their blood upon their heads.
FERNEZE
    Then take them up, and let them be interred
    Within one sacred monument of stone;   30
    Upon which altar I will offer up
    My daily sacrifice of sighs and tears,

17 *leave* cease
18 *lively* life-giving

And with my prayers pierce impartial heavens,
Till they [reveal] the causers of our smarts,
Which forced their hands divide united hearts: 35
Come, Katherine, our losses equal are,
Then of true grief let us take equal share.

Exeunt [*with the bodies*]

[Act III, Scene iii]

Enter ITHAMORE

ITHAMORE
Why, was there ever seen such villainy,
So neatly plotted, and so well performed?
Both held in hand, and flatly both beguiled.

Enter ABIGAIL

ABIGAIL
Why how now Ithamore, why laugh'st thou so?
ITHAMORE
Oh, mistress, ha ha ha.   5
ABIGAIL
Why what ail'st thou?
ITHAMORE
Oh my master.
ABIGAIL
Ha.
ITHAMORE
Oh mistress! I have the bravest, gravest, secret, subtle,
bottle-nosed knave to my master, that ever gentleman   10
had.

---

33 *impartial* indifferent
34 *reveal* Most editors follow Dyce in assuming some such word to be omitted here.
   smarts pains, injuries
 1–3 ed. (Q neatly / Plotted ... and / Flatly)
   Why, was ed. (Q Why was)
 3 *held in hand* falsely encouraged
   flatly completely, utterly
 6 *what ail'st thou* what is wrong with you?
 9 *bravest* finest, most impressive
10–11 ed. (Q *one line*)
10 *bottle-nosed* swollen, bottle-shaped
   to for
11 *had.* ed. (Q had)

ABIGAIL

Say, knave, why rail'st upon my father thus?

ITHAMORE

Oh, my master has the bravest policy.

ABIGAIL

Wherein?

ITHAMORE

Why, know you not?   15

ABIGAIL

Why no.

ITHAMORE

Know you not of Mathias' and Don Lodowick's disaster?

ABIGAIL

No, what was it?

ITHAMORE

Why the devil invented a challenge, my master writ it,
and I carried it, first to Lodowick, and *imprimis* to   20
Mathias.
And then they met, and as the story says,
In doleful wise they ended both their days.

ABIGAIL

And was my father furtherer of their deaths?

ITHAMORE

Am I Ithamore?   25

ABIGAIL

Yes.

ITHAMORE

So sure did your father write, and I carry the challenge.

ABIGAIL

Well, Ithamore, let me request thee this,
Go to the new-made nunnery, and inquire
For any of the friars of St Jacques,   30
And say, I pray them come and speak with me.

12 *rail'st upon* abuse, mock
17 *Mathias' ... Lodowick's* ed. (Q Mathia & Don Lodowick)
20–1 ed. (Q *one line*)
20 *imprimis* (Latin) first (Ithamore's error). See his mistaken usage at IV.ii.100.
22 *met, and as* ed. (Q met, as)
23 *In ... days* Ithamore's deliberately archaic, literary diction, like his obvious
delight in 'such villainy ... neatly plotted', his misused Latin and his laughter are
reminders of his relation to the Vice figure of the earlier stage.
24 *furtherer* agent
30 *Jacques* ed. (Q Iaynes) Dominican friars, named after their church of St Jaques
in Paris

ITHAMORE

  I pray, mistress, will you answer me to one question?

ABIGAIL

  Well, sirrah, what is't?

ITHAMORE

  A very feeling one; have not the nuns fine sport with the
  friars now and then?   35

ABIGAIL

  Go to, sirrah sauce, is this your question? Get ye gone.

ITHAMORE

  I will forsooth, mistress.   *Exit*

ABIGAIL

  Hard-hearted father, unkind Barabas,
  Was this the pursuit of thy policy?
  To make me show them favour severally,   40
  That by my favour they should both be slain?
  Admit thou lovedst not Lodowick for his sin,
  Yet Don Mathias ne'er offended thee:
  But thou wert set upon extreme revenge,
  Because the Prior dispossessed thee once,   45
  And couldst not venge it, but upon his son,
  Nor on his son, but by Mathias' means;
  Nor on Mathias, but by murdering me.
  But I perceive there is no love on earth,
  Pity in Jews, nor piety in Turks.   50
  But here comes cursed Ithamore with the friar.

Enter ITHAMORE, FRIAR [JACOMO]

JACOMO

  Virgo, salve.

34–5 ed. (Q A ... sport / With ... then?)

34 *a very feeling one* a deeply emotional one (with ironic play on 'feeling' in a physical
    sense)

36 *go to, sirrah sauce* enough, impudent fellow
    gone. ed. (Q gon)

38 *unkind* unfeeling and/or unnatural

39 *pursuit* direction, outcome

40 *severally* separately

42 Q's *sinne* is frequently amended to read 'sire', since Lodowick himself has not
    harmed Barabas, but the attention of the play to assumptions about morality and
    inherited guilt gives Q's wording some claim to interest.

45 *Prior* governing official

52 *Virgo, salve* (Latin) Greetings (God save you), maiden

ITHAMORE
  When, duck you?
ABIGAIL
  Welcome grave friar: Ithamore be gone.

Exit [ITHAMORE]
  Know, holy sir, I am bold to solicit thee.   55
JACOMO
  Wherein?
ABIGAIL
  To get me be admitted for a nun.
JACOMO
  Why Abigail it is not yet long since
  That I did labour thy admission,
  And then thou didst not like that holy life.   60
ABIGAIL
  Then were my thoughts so frail and unconfirmed,
  And I was chained to follies of the world:
  But now experience, purchasèd with grief,
  Has made me see the difference of things.
  My sinful soul, alas, hath paced too long   65
  The fatal labyrinth of misbelief,
  Far from the Son that gives eternal life.
JACOMO
  Who taught thee this?
ABIGAIL   The abbess of the house,
  Whose zealous admonition I embrace:
  Oh therefore, Jacomo, let me be one,   70
  Although unworthy of that sisterhood.
JACOMO
  Abigail I will, but see thou change no more,
  For that will be most heavy to thy soul.
ABIGAIL
  That was my father's fault.
JACOMO   Thy father's, how?

---

53 *When, duck you?* ed. (Q When ducke you?) Do you bow? 'When' expresses
   impatience.
57 *To get me be admitted for* to procure my admission as
59 *labour* labour for
61 *unconfirmed* unsettled, unsolidified
67 *Son* ed. (Q Sonne) possibly punning on 'sun' and 'son'
69 *admonition* teaching, counsel
70 *Jacomo* ed. (Q *Iacomi*)
73 *heavy* grievous

ABIGAIL
  Nay, you shall pardon me. (Oh Barabas,   75
  Though thou deservest hardly at my hands,
  Yet never shall these lips bewray thy life.)
JACOMO
  Come, shall we go?
ABIGAIL   My duty waits on you.

                                                 Exeunt

[Act III, Scene iv]

Enter BARABAS *reading a letter*

BARABAS
  What, Abigail become a nun again?
  False, and unkind; what, hast thou lost thy father?
  And all unknown, and unconstrained of me,
  Art thou again got to the nunnery?
  Now here she writes, and wills me to repent.   5
  Repentance? *Spurca*: what pretendeth this?
  I fear she knows – 'tis so – of my device
  In Don Mathias' and Lodovico's deaths:
  If so, 'tis time that it be seen into:
  For she that varies from me in belief   10
  Gives great presumption that she loves me not;
  Or loving, doth dislike of something done.
  But who comes here?

               [*Enter* ITHAMORE]

             Oh Ithamore come near;
  Come near my love, come near thy master's life,
  My trusty servant, nay, my second life;   15

---

75 ed. (Q Nay, you shall pardon me: oh *Barabas*,)
76 *hardly* severely
77 *bewray* betray
 2 *unkind* unnatural (cf. III.iii.38)
  what, hast ed. (Q what hast)
 6 *Spurca* (Italian) filthy
  pretendeth signifies
 7 ed. (Q I feare she knowes ('tis so) of my deuice)
 9 *seen into* looked to
11 *presumption* grounds for presuming
15 *life* Many editions change Q's reading to 'self'.

For I have now no hope but even in thee;
And on that hope my happiness is built:
When saw'st thou Abigail?

ITHAMORE
Today.

BARABAS
With whom?   20

ITHAMORE
A friar.

BARABAS
A friar? False villain, he hath done the deed.

ITHAMORE
How, sir?

BARABAS
Why made mine Abigail a nun.

ITHAMORE
That's no lie, for she sent me for him.   25

BARABAS
O unhappy day,
False, credulous, inconstant Abigail!
But let 'em go: and Ithamore, from hence
Ne'er shall she grieve me more with her disgrace;
Ne'er shall she live to inherit aught of mine,   30
Be blest of me, nor come within my gates,
But perish underneath my bitter curse
Like Cain by Adam, for his brother's death.

ITHAMORE
Oh master.

BARABAS
Ithamore, entreat not for her, I am moved,   35
And she is hateful to my soul and me:
And 'less thou yield to this that I entreat,
I cannot think but that thou hatest my life.

ITHAMORE
Who I, master? Why I'll run to some rock and throw
myself headlong into the sea; why I'll do anything for   40
your sweet sake.

31 *come within my gates* another of the play's many biblical phrasings (see, e.g.,
Deuteronomy 17.2)

33 *Like Cain by Adam* As elsewhere, Barabas's use of familiar biblical or classical
sources is pointedly ironic or inaccurate. Cain was cursed by God, not by his
father Adam, for killing his brother, and, despite the curse, lived under God's
protection (Genesis 4).

35 *moved* emotionally upset

37 *'less* ed. (Q least) unless

39–41 ed. (Q Who ... and / Throw ... any / Thing ... sake.)

BARABAS

   Oh trusty Ithamore; no servant, but my friend;
   I here adopt thee for mine only heir,
   All that I have is thine when I am dead,
   And whilst I live use half; spend as myself;   45
   Here take my keys, I'll give 'em thee anon:
   Go buy thee garments: but thou shalt not want:
   Only know this, that thus thou art to do:
   But first go fetch me in the pot of rice
   That for our supper stands upon the fire.   50

ITHAMORE

   (I hold my head my master's hungry.) I go sir.   *Exit*

BARABAS

   Thus every villain ambles after wealth
   Although he ne'er be richer than in hope:
   But husht.

Enter ITHAMORE *with the pot*

ITHAMORE

   Here 'tis, master.   55

BARABAS

   Well said, Ithamore; what, hast thou brought the ladle
   with thee too?

ITHAMORE

   Yes, sir, the proverb says, he that eats with the devil had
   need of a long spoon, I have brought you a ladle.

BARABAS

   Very well, Ithamore, then now be secret;   60
   And for thy sake, whom I so dearly love,
   Now shalt thou see the death of Abigail,
   That thou mayst freely live to be my heir.

46–7 Apparently Barabas offers, but does not actually give, Ithamore the keys and
    wealth he promises.
48 *thus thou art to do* this is what you will be able to do
51 *(I . . . hungry.) I* ed. (Q I . . . hungry: I)
   hold wager
52 *ambles* paces
54 *husht* ed. (Q hush't) be silent
56–7 ed. (Q Well . . . brought / The . . . too?)
56 *what,* ed. (Q what)
58–9 ed. (Q Yes . . . deuil / Had . . . Ladle.)

ITHAMORE

    Why, master, will you poison her with a mess of rice
    porridge that will preserve life, make her round and   65
    plump, and batten more than you are aware?

BARABAS

    Ay but Ithamore seest thou this?
    It is a precious powder that I bought
    Of an Italian in Ancona once,
    Whose operation is to bind, infect,   70
    And poison deeply: yet not appear
    In forty hours after it is ta'en.

ITHAMORE

    How master?

BARABAS

    Thus Ithamore:
    This even they use in Malta here – 'tis called   75
    Saint Jacques' Even – and then I say they use
    To send their alms unto the nunneries:
    Among the rest bear this, and set it there;
    There's a dark entry where they take it in,
    Where they must neither see the messenger,   80
    Nor make enquiry who hath sent it them.

ITHAMORE

    How so?

BARABAS

    Belike there is some ceremony in't.
    There Ithamore must thou go place this pot:
    Stay, let me spice it first.   85

ITHAMORE

    Pray do, and let me help you master. Pray let me taste
    first.

64 *mess* serving

65–6 ed. (Q Porredge ... plump, / And ... aware.)

66 *batten* grow fat

    aware? ed. (Q aware.)

69 *Ancona* an Italian port with a history of tolerance towards Jews until their forced
    conversion or expulsion on papal orders in 1556

70 *bind* constipate

75 *This even they use* this evening they are accustomed to

75–6 *here – 'tis called / Saint Jacques' Even – and* ed. (Q here ('tis call'd / Saint *Iagues*
    Euen) and)

83 *belike* perhaps

    ceremony customary observance

84 *pot* ed.(Q plot)

86–7 ed. (Q *one line*)

BARABAS

Prithee do: what say'st thou now?

ITHAMORE

Troth master, I'm loath such a pot of pottage should be
spoiled.   90

BARABAS

Peace, Ithamore, 'tis better so than spared.

[BARABAS *puts in poison*]

Assure thyself thou shalt have broth by the eye.
My purse, my coffer, and my self is thine.

ITHAMORE

Well, master, I go.

BARABAS

Stay, first let me stir it Ithamore.   95
As fatal be it to her as the draught
Of which great Alexander drunk, and died:
And with her let it work like Borgia's wine,
Whereof his sire, the Pope, was poisonèd.
In few, the blood of Hydra, Lerna's bane;   100
The juice of hebon, and Cocytus' breath,
And all the poisons of the Stygian pool
Break from the fiery kingdom; and in this
Vomit your venom, and envenom her
That like a fiend hath left her father thus.   105

ITHAMORE

What a blessing has he given't! Was ever pot of rice
porridge so sauced? What shall I do with it?

89–90 ed. (Q *one line*)
89 *Troth* in truth, by my faith
   pottage soup
92 *by the eye* abundantly
97 *great Alexander* One story of Alexander the Great's death (told by Plutarch,
   among others) held that he was poisoned.
98 *Borgia's wine* Cesare Borgia was reputed to have poisoned his father, Pope
   Alexander VI, in 1503.
100 *in few* in short
   Hydra, Lerna's bane the nine-headed monster slain by Hercules that was troub-
   ling to Lerna, near Argos, and whose blood was poisonous
101 *hebon* a poisonous plant, perhaps the yew
   Cocytus one of the rivers of Hades
102 *Stygian* referring to the Styx, the principal river of Hades
106–7 ed. (Q What ... of / Rice ... it?)
107 *sauced* seasoned

BARABAS

Oh my sweet Ithamore go set it down
And come again so soon as thou hast done,
For I have other business for thee.   110

ITHAMORE

Here's a drench to poison a whole stable of Flanders
mares: I'll carry't to the nuns with a powder.

BARABAS

And the horse pestilence to boot; away.

ITHAMORE

I am gone.
Pay me my wages for my work is done.   *Exit* 115

BARABAS

I'll pay thee with a vengeance Ithamore.   *Exit*

[Act III, Scene v]

Enter GOVERNOR [FERNEZE], [MARTIN DEL] BOSCO,
KNIGHTS, BASHAW

FERNEZE

Welcome great Bashaw, how fares Calymath,
What wind drives you thus into Malta road?

BASHAW

The wind that bloweth all the world besides,
Desire of gold.

FERNEZE   Desire of gold, great sir?
That's to be gotten in the Western Ind: 5
In Malta are no golden minerals.

BASHAW

To you of Malta thus saith Calymath:
The time you took for respite is at hand,
For the performance of your promise past;
And for the tribute-money I am sent.   10

111–12 ed. (Q Here's . . . of / Flanders . . . powder.)
111 *drench* medicinal dose
     Flanders mares Belgian horses or lascivious women
112 *with a powder* quickly and/or with the powdered poison
113 *horse pestilence* unclear: apparently some horse disease
     to boot besides
116 *with a vengeance* to an extreme degree and/or with a curse
  1 *Bashaw* ed. (Q *Bashaws*)
  2 As Craik points out, the stress on 'you' here helps to create a sense of Ferneze's
     surprise as feigned; he well knows why the Bashaw has come.
  5 *Western Ind* the Western Hemisphere
  8 *respite is* ed. (Q respite, is)

FERNEZE
  Bashaw, in brief, shalt have no tribute here,
  Nor shall the heathens live upon our spoil:
  First will we race the city walls ourselves,
  Lay waste the island, hew the temples down,
  And shipping of our goods to Sicily,   15
  Open an entrance for the wasteful sea,
  Whose billows beating the resistless banks,
  Shall overflow it with their refluence.
BASHAW
  Well, Governor, since thou hast broke the league
  By flat denial of the promised tribute,   20
  Talk not of racing down your city walls,
  You shall not need trouble yourselves so far,
  For Selim-Calymath shall come himself,
  And with brass bullets batter down your towers,
  And turn proud Malta to a wilderness   25
  For these intolerable wrongs of yours;
  And so farewell.   [*Exit*]
FERNEZE
  Farewell:
  And now you men of Malta look about,
  And let's provide to welcome Calymath: 30
  Close your portcullis, charge your basilisks,
  And as you profitably take up arms,
  So now courageously encounter them;
  For by this answer, broken is the league,
  And nought is to be looked for now but wars,   35
  And nought to us more welcome is than wars.
                                      Exeunt

---

13 *race* raze
15 *of* Many editors amend to 'off'.
18 *refluence* flowing back
26–7 ed. (Q *one line*)
31 *portcullis* a grid-like structure which could be lowered to block a gateway
    basilisks large cannon
32 *profitably* beneficially. The sense of more financial sorts of 'profit' is also possible.

[Act III, Scene vi]

Enter two FRIARS [JACOMO *and* BERNARDINE]

JACOMO
  Oh brother, brother, all the nuns are sick,
  And physic will not help them; they must die.
BERNARDINE
  The abbess sent for me to be confessed:
  Oh what a sad confession will there be!
JACOMO
  And so did fair Maria send for me: 5
  I'll to her lodging; hereabouts she lies.   *Exit*

Enter ABIGAIL

BERNARDINE
  What, all dead save only Abigail?
ABIGAIL
  And I shall die too, for I feel death coming.
  Where is the friar that conversed with me?
BERNARDINE
  Oh he is gone to see the other nuns.   10
ABIGAIL
  I sent for him, but seeing you are come
  Be you my ghostly father; and first know,
  That in this house I lived religiously,
  Chaste and devout, much sorrowing for my sins,
  But ere I came –   15
BERNARDINE
  What then?
ABIGAIL
  I did offend high heaven so grievously,
  As I am almost desperate for my sins:
  And one offence torments me more than all.
  You knew Mathias and Don Lodowick?   20
BERNARDINE
  Yes, what of them?

0.1 ed. (Q *Enter two Fryars and Abigall.*)

1–3 *Jacomo . . . Bernardine* ed. (Q *1 Fry . . . 2 Fry*)

2 *physic* medicine

4 *be!* ed. (Q be?) The question mark in Elizabethan texts often simply registers
  emphasis, not interrogation.

12 *ghostly father* spiritual confessor

18 *desperate* despairing of salvation

ABIGAIL

My father did contract me to 'em both:
First to Don Lodowick, him I never loved;
Mathias was the man that I held dear,
And for his sake did I become a nun.   25

BERNARDINE

So, say how was their end?

ABIGAIL

Both jealous of my love, envied each other:
And by my father's practice, which is there
Set down at large, the gallants were both slain.

                        [*Gives a paper*]

BERNARDINE

Oh monstrous villainy!   30

ABIGAIL

To work my peace, this I confess to thee;
Reveal it not, for then my father dies.

BERNARDINE

Know that confession must not be revealed,
The canon law forbids it, and the priest
That makes it known, being degraded first,   35
Shall be condemned, and then sent to the fire.

ABIGAIL

So I have heard; pray therefore keep it close,
Death seizeth on my heart, ah gentle friar
Convert my father that he may be saved,
And witness that I die a Christian.   [*Dies*]   40

BERNARDINE

Ay, and a virgin too, that grieves me most:
But I must to the Jew and exclaim on him,
And make him stand in fear of me.

                    Enter FRIAR [JACOMO]

22 *contract* promise, betroth
28 *practice* contrivance, treachery
29 *set down at large* written out at length
30 *villainy!* ed. (Q villany:)
31 *work my peace* win my absolution
36 *sent to the fire* Bawcutt points out that penalty and possible excommunication
   might follow such violation of canon law, but the death penalty twice mentioned
   here for violating confessional confidentiality is apparently Marlowe's exag-
   geration.
37 *close* secret
42 *exclaim upon* denounce

JACOMO
    Oh brother, all the nuns are dead, let's bury them.
BERNARDINE
    First help to bury this, then go with me   45
    And help me to exclaim against the Jew.
JACOMO
    Why? What has he done?
BERNARDINE
    A thing that makes me tremble to unfold.
JACOMO
    What, has he crucified a child?
BERNARDINE
    No, but a worse thing: 'twas told me in shrift,   50
    Thou know'st 'tis death and if it be revealed.
    Come let's away.

                           Exeunt [with the body]

Act IV [Scene i]

Enter BARABAS, ITHAMORE. *Bells within*

BARABAS
    There is no music to a Christian's knell:
    How sweet the bells ring now the nuns are dead
    That sound at other times like tinkers' pans!
    I was afraid the poison had not wrought;
    Or though it wrought, it would have done no good,   5
    For every year they swell, and yet they live;
    Now all are dead, not one remains alive.
ITHAMORE
    That's brave, master, but think you it will not be known?

---

  49 *What,* ed. (Q What)
     crucified a child One traditional legend of anti-Semitism held that Jews crucified
     Christian children.
  50 *shrift* confession
   1 *to* comparable to
   3 *pans!* ed. (Q pans?)
   4 *wrought* worked
   6 *swell* i.e. from pregnancy
   8 *brave* fine
    known? ed. (Q has no end punctuation)

BARABAS
How can it if we two be secret?
ITHAMORE
For my part fear you not. 10
BARABAS
I'd cut thy throat if I did.
ITHAMORE
And reason too;
But here's a royal monastery hard by,
Good master let me poison all the monks.
BARABAS
Thou shalt not need, for now the nuns are dead, 15
They'll die with grief.
ITHAMORE
Do you not sorrow for your daughter's death?
BARABAS
No, but I grieve because she lived so long
An Hebrew born, and would become a Christian.
Cazzo, diavola. 20

Enter the TWO FRIARS [JACOMO *and* BERNARDINE]

ITHAMORE
Look, look, master, here come two religious caterpillars.
BARABAS
I smelt 'em ere they came.
ITHAMORE
(God-a-mercy nose.) Come let's be gone.
BERNARDINE
Stay wicked Jew, repent, I say, and stay.
JACOMO
Thou hast offended, therefore must be damned. 25
BARABAS
I fear they know we sent the poisoned broth.
ITHAMORE
And so do I, master, therefore speak 'em fair.

9 *secret?* ed. (Q secret.)
12 *and reason too* and with reason too
12–14 ed. (Q And ... Hard / By ... Monks.)
13 *royal* fine, splendid
18–19 ed. (Q No ... *Hebrew* / Borne ... *diabola.*) Many editors add punctuation after 'long'.
20 *Cazzo, diavola* ed. (Q (marginally) *Catho diabola*); probably an oath derived from Italian 'cazzo' for 'penis' and 'diavola' for female devil
21 *caterpillars* parasites upon the social order
23 ed. (Q God-a-mercy nose; come let's begone.)
   God-a-mercy nose thanks to your big nose

BERNARDINE
  Barabas, thou hast –
JACOMO
  Ay, that thou hast –
BARABAS
  True, I have money, what though I have?   30
BERNARDINE
  Thou art a –
JACOMO
  Ay, that thou art, a –
BARABAS
  What needs all this? I know I am a Jew.
BERNARDINE
  Thy daughter –
JACOMO
  Ay, thy daughter –   35
BARABAS
  Oh speak not of her, then I die with grief.
BERNARDINE
  Remember that –
JACOMO
  Ay, remember that –
BARABAS
  I must needs say that I have been a great usurer.
BERNARDINE
  Thou hast committed –
BARABAS   Fornication?   40
  But that was in another country:
  And besides, the wench is dead.
BERNARDINE
  Ay, but Barabas remember Mathias and Don Lodowick.
BARABAS
  Why, what of them?
BERNARDINE
  I will not say that by a forged challenge they met.   45
BARABAS
  (She has confessed, and we are both undone;)
  My bosom inmates (but I must dissemble).

28–40 For a useful consideration of the implications of Barabas's adoption of the
    discourse of anti-Semitism, see Hodge.

40–2 ed. (Q Fornication ... Country: / And ... dead.)

46–7 Q marks 47 '*aside*' and uses italics for 'but I must dissemble' perhaps to signal
    Barabas's progress from conspiratorial aside ('we are both undone') to an address
    to the friars ('My bosom inmates'), to an aside possibly unheard by anyone on-
    stage ('*but I must dissemble*').

Oh holy friars, the burden of my sins
Lie heavy on my soul; then pray you tell me,
Is't not too late now to turn Christian?   50
I have been zealous in the Jewish faith,
Hard-hearted to the poor, a covetous wretch,
That would for lucre's sake have sold my soul.
A hundred for a hundred I have ta'en;
And now for store of wealth may I compare   55
With all the Jews in Malta; but what is wealth?
I am a Jew, and therefore am I lost.
Would penance serve for this my sin,
I could afford to whip myself to death.

ITHAMORE

And so could I; but penance will not serve.   60

BARABAS

To fast, to pray, and wear a shirt of hair,
And on my knees creep to Jerusalem.
Cellars of wine, and sollars full of wheat,
Warehouses stuffed with spices and with drugs,
Whole chests of gold, in bullion, and in coin,   65
Besides I know not how much weight in pearl
Orient and round, have I within my house;
At Alexandria, merchandise unsold:
But yesterday two ships went from this town,
Their voyage will be worth ten thousand crowns.   70
In Florence, Venice, Antwerp, London, Seville,
Frankfurt, Lubeck, Moscow, and where not,
Have I debts owing; and in most of these,
Great sums of money lying in the banco;
All this I'll give to some religious house   75
So I may be baptized and live therein.

JACOMO

Oh good Barabas come to our house.

---

53 *lucre's* wealth's
54 *A hundred for a hundred* one hundred per cent interest
58 *serve for* serve to atone for
60 Whether or not Ithamore understands Barabas's strategic hypocrisy here, he is
   characteristically uninterested in suffering.
62 *Jerusalem.* ed. (Q *Ierusalem,*)
63 *sollars* lofts
64 *drugs* medicines
65 *bullion* ed. (Q *Bulloine* i.e. Boulogne)
67 *Orient* precious, lustrous
70 *crowns.* ed. (Q crowns)
74 *banco* bank

BERNARDINE
Oh no, good Barabas come to our house.
And Barabas, you know –
BARABAS
I know that I have highly sinned,   80
You shall convert me, you shall have all my wealth.
JACOMO
Oh Barabas, their laws are strict.
BARABAS
I know they are, and I will be with you.
BERNARDINE
They wear no shirts, and they go barefoot too.
BARABAS
Then 'tis not for me; and I am resolved   85
You shall confess me, and have all my goods.
JACOMO
Good Barabas come to me.
BARABAS
You see I answer him, and yet he stays;
Rid him away, and go you home with me.
BERNARDINE
I'll be with you tonight.   90
BARABAS
Come to my house at one o'clock this night.
JACOMO
You hear your answer, and you may be gone.
BERNARDINE
Why go get you away.
JACOMO
I will not go for thee.
BERNARDINE
Not, then I'll make thee go.   95
JACOMO
How, dost call me rogue?   *Fight*
ITHAMORE
Part 'em, master, part 'em.
BARABAS
This is mere frailty, brethren, be content.

84–96 The assignment of the friars' speeches has long been a problem; most modern
     editors award line 84 to Bernardine rather than to Q's '1 [Friar]', i.e. Jacomo.
     On the basis of lines 103–5 Craik argues compellingly that Bernardine must have
     made critical remarks about the Dominicans in this passage. In any case the
     thrust of the passage is that each friar naively believes himself in favour with
     Barabas and, hence, in line for his wealth.

Friar Bernardine go you with Ithamore.
You know my mind, let me alone with him.   100
JACOMO
Why does he go to thy house, let him be gone.
BARABAS
I'll give him something and so stop his mouth.
                    [*Exeunt* ITHAMORE *and* FRIAR BERNARDINE]
I never heard of any man but he
Maligned the order of the Jacobins:
But do you think that I believe his words?   105
Why brother you converted Abigail;
And I am bound in charity to requite it,
And so I will, oh Jacomo, fail not but come.
JACOMO
But Barabas who shall be your godfathers?
For presently you shall be shrived.   110
BARABAS
Marry the Turk shall be one of my godfathers,
But not a word to any of your covent.
JACOMO
I warrant thee, Barabas.   *Exit*
BARABAS
So now the fear is past, and I am safe:
For he that shrived her is within my house.   115
What if I murdered him ere Jacomo comes?
Now I have such a plot for both their lives,
As never Jew nor Christian knew the like:
One turned my daughter, therefore he shall die;
The other knows enough to have my life,   120
Therefore 'tis not requisite he should live.
But are not both these wise men to suppose
That I will leave my house, my goods, and all,

100–1 Q gives both lines to Ithamore. Recent editors assume line 100 is intended to
        reassure Bernardine, but Bawcutt points out it is possible that 'let me alone with
        him' could be Ithamore's response to Barabas's own prompting – 'You know my
        mind.'
102 s.d. ed. (Q *Exit*)
104 *Jacobins* Dominicans (see III.iii.30)
109 *godfathers?* ed. (Q godfathers,)
110 *shrived* confessed
111 *the Turk* Ithamore
112 *covent* community, convent
113 *I warrant thee* I give you my promise
115 *house.* ed. (Q house,)
119 *turned* converted
121 *'tis not requisite . . . live* ironic understatement: 'it is not necessary that he live'

To fast and be well whipped; I'll none of that.
Now Friar Bernardine I come to you,   125
I'll feast you, lodge you, give you fair words,
And after that, I and my trusty Turk –
No more but so: it must and shall be done.
Ithamore, tell me, is the friar asleep?

Enter ITHAMORE

ITHAMORE
   Yes; and I know not what the reason is: 130
   Do what I can he will not strip himself,
   Nor go to bed, but sleeps in his own clothes;
   I fear me he mistrusts what we intend.
BARABAS
   No, 'tis an order which the friars use:
   Yet if he knew our meanings, could he 'scape?   135
ITHAMORE
   No, none can hear him, cry he ne'er so loud.
BARABAS
   Why true, therefore did I place him there:
   The other chambers open towards the street.
ITHAMORE
   You loiter, master, wherefore stay we thus?
   Oh how I long to see him shake his heels.   140

[*Discovers* FRIAR BERNARDINE *asleep*]

BARABAS
   Come on, sirrah,
   Off with your girdle, make a handsome noose;
   Friar awake.
BERNARDINE
   What do you mean to strangle me?
ITHAMORE
   Yes, 'cause you use to confess.   145

---

128 *No more but so* just so, without further ado
133 *mistrusts* suspects
134 *order* customary observance
135 *meanings* intentions
139 *stay* delay
140 *shake his heels* i.e. when he is hanged
141–2 ed. (Q *one line*)
142 *girdle* belt
145 *use to confess* make a practice of hearing (and making) confessions; punning on
    religious and judicial meanings

BARABAS

Blame not us but the proverb, 'Confess and be hanged'.
Pull hard.

BERNARDINE

What, will you have my life?

BARABAS

Pull hard, I say, you would have had my goods.

ITHAMORE

Ay, and our lives too, therefore pull amain.   150
'Tis neatly done, sir, here's no print at all.

BARABAS

Then is it as it should be, take him up.

ITHAMORE

Nay, master, be ruled by me a little; so, let him lean
upon his staff; excellent, he stands as if he were begging
of bacon.   155

BARABAS

Who would not think but that this friar lived?
What time o' night is't now, sweet Ithamore?

ITHAMORE

Towards one.

Enter [FRIAR] JACOMO

BARABAS

Then will not Jacomo be long from hence.
                    [*Exeunt* BARABAS *and* ITHAMORE]

JACOMO

This is the hour wherein I shall proceed;   160
Oh happy hour, wherein I shall convert
An infidel, and bring his gold into our treasury.
But soft, is not this Bernardine? It is;
And understanding I should come this way,
Stands here o' purpose, meaning me some wrong,   165
And intercept my going to the Jew;
Bernardine!
Wilt thou not speak? Thou think'st I see thee not;

148 *have* ed. (Q saue)
150 *amain* strongly
151 *print* mark on his neck left by the noose
152 *take him up* pick him up and remove him
153 *Nay . . . so* Ithamore stands the friar up as he speaks.
154–5 ed. (Q *one line*)
160 *proceed* prosper
163 *But soft* but wait a moment
166 *intercept* to intercept
166–8 ed. (Q And . . . *Bernardine*; / Wilt . . . not;)

Away, I'd wish thee, and let me go by:
No, wilt thou not? Nay then I'll force my way;   170
And see, a staff stands ready for the purpose:
As thou lik'st that, stop me another time.

> *Strike[s] him, he falls. Enter* BARABAS [*and*
> ITHAMORE]

BARABAS
Why how now Jacomo, what hast thou done?
JACOMO
Why stricken him that would have struck at me.
BARABAS
Who is it, Bernardine? Now out alas, he is slain.   175
ITHAMORE
Ay, master, he's slain; look how his brains drop out on's
nose.
JACOMO
Good sirs I have done't, but nobody knows it but you
two, I may escape.
BARABAS
So might my man and I hang with you for company.   180
ITHAMORE
No, let us bear him to the magistrates.
JACOMO
Good Barabas let me go.
BARABAS
No, pardon me, the law must have his course.
I must be forced to give in evidence,
That being importuned by this Bernardine   185
To be a Christian, I shut him out,
And there he sat: now I to keep my word,
And give my goods and substance to your house,
Was up thus early; with intent to go
Unto your friary, because you stayed.   190
ITHAMORE
Fie upon 'em, master, will you turn Christian, when holy
friars turn devils and murder one another?

175 *it, Bernardine?* ed. (Q *it Bernardine?*)
    out alas an expression of horror
176–7 ed. (Q *one line*)
176 *on's* of his
178–9 ed. (Q Good ... but / You ... escape.)
183 *his* its
185 *importuned* solicited
190 *stayed* delayed coming
191–2 ed. (Q Fie ... when / Holy ... another.)   192 *another?* ed. (Q another.)

BARABAS

No, for this example I'll remain a Jew:
Heaven bless me; what, a friar a murderer?
When shall you see a Jew commit the like?   195

ITHAMORE

Why a Turk could ha' done no more.

BARABAS

Tomorrow is the sessions; you shall to it.
Come Ithamore, let's help to take him hence.

JACOMO

Villains, I am a sacred person, touch me not.

BARABAS

The law shall touch you, we'll but lead you, we: 200
'Las I could weep at your calamity.
Take in the staff too, for that must be shown:
Law wills that each particular be known.

Exeunt

[Act IV, Scene ii]

Enter COURTESAN [BELLAMIRA] *and* PILIA-BORZA

BELLAMIRA

Pilia-Borza, didst thou meet with Ithamore?

PILIA-BORZA

I did.

BELLAMIRA

And didst thou deliver my letter?

PILIA-BORZA

I did.

BELLAMIRA

And what think'st thou, will he come?   5

PILIA-BORZA

I think so, and yet I cannot tell, for at the reading of the
letter, he looked like a man of another world.

BELLAMIRA

Why so?

197 *sessions* when the court sits
201 *'Las* Alas
203 *wills* demands
   particular piece of evidence
   6–7 ed. (Q I ... of / The ... world.)
   7 *man of another world* spirit

PILIA-BORZA

That such a base slave as he should be saluted by such a
tall man as I am, from such a beautiful dame as you.   10

BELLAMIRA

And what said he?

PILIA-BORZA

Not a wise word, only gave me a nod, as who should say,
'Is it even so?' And so I left him, being driven to a non-
plus at the critical aspect of my terrible countenance.

BELLAMIRA

And where didst meet him?   15

PILIA-BORZA

Upon mine own freehold within forty foot of the gallows,
conning his neck verse I take it, looking of a friar's
execution, whom I saluted with an old hempen proverb,
Hodie tibi, cras mihi, and so I left him to the mercy of the
hangman: but the exercise being done, see where he   20
comes.

Enter ITHAMORE

ITHAMORE

I never knew a man take his death so patiently as this
friar; he was ready to leap off ere the halter was about
his neck; and when the hangman had put on his hempen
tippet, he made such haste to his prayers, as if he had   25

9–10 ed. (Q That ... such / A ... you.)
9 *saluted* addressed
10 *tall* brave, splendid
13 *even so?' And* ed. (Q euen so; and)
13–14 *non-plus* state of perplexity
16–21 ed. (Q Vpon ... the / Gallowes ... a / Fryars ... hempen / prouerb ... mercy
  / Of ... where / He comes.)
16 *freehold* literally, land held as private estate; here perhaps the location of Pilia-
  Borza's career as pickpocket
17 *conning* studying
  neck verse the Latin verse (generally Psalm 51) that the criminal must be able to
  read in order to claim 'benefit of clergy' and thereby escape punishment
  looking of looking at
18 *hempen* referring to the hangman's rope
19 *Hodie ... mihi* ed. (Q *Hidie ... mihi*); (Latin) today you; tomorrow me
20 *exercise being done* religious service being over
22–38 ed. (Q I ... as / This ... was / About ... his / Hempen ... if / Hee ... whither
  / He ... haste: / And ... fellow / Met ... and / A ... he / Gaue ... *Bellamira*, /
  Saluting ... make / Cleane ... that / I ... is; / It ... in / My ... me / Euer ... such
  / Loue ... now / Would ... her.)
25 *tippet* the scarf worn around a priest's neck

had another cure to serve; well, go whither he will, I'll
be none of his followers in haste: and now I think on't,
going to the execution, a fellow met me with a muschatoes like a raven's wing, and a dagger with a hilt like
a warming-pan, and he gave me a letter from one Madam   30
Bellamira, saluting me in such sort as if he had meant to
make clean my boots with his lips; the effect was, that I
should come to her house, I wonder what the reason is;
it may be she sees more in me than I can find in myself:
for she writes further, that she loves me ever since she   35
saw me, and who would not requite such love? Here's
her house, and here she comes, and now would I were
gone, I am not worthy to look upon her.

PILIA-BORZA

This is the gentleman you writ to.

ITHAMORE

('Gentleman', he flouts me, what gentry can be in a poor   40
Turk of ten pence? I'll be gone.)

BELLAMIRA

Is't not a sweet-faced youth, Pilia?

ITHAMORE

(Again, 'sweet youth'.) Did not you, sir, bring the sweet
youth a letter?

PILIA-BORZA

I did sir, and from this gentlewoman, who as myself,   45
and the rest of the family, stand or fall at your service.

BELLAMIRA

Though woman's modesty should hale me back,
I can withhold no longer; welcome sweet love.

ITHAMORE

(Now am I clean, or rather foully out of the way.)

BELLAMIRA

Whither so soon?   50

---

26 *cure to serve* parish to minister to
28 *muschatoes* moustache
40–1 ed. (Q Gentleman . . . a / Poore . . . gone.)
40 *flouts* mocks
41 *Turk of ten pence* i.e. worthless person
43–4 ed. (Q Agen sweet youth; did not you, Sir, bring the sweet / Youth a letter?)
45–6 ed. (Q I . . . my / Selfe . . . seruice.)
46 *family* household
47 *hale* pull
49 *clean* completely (with a pun contrasting 'foully')
   out of the way out of my depth; bewildered

ITHAMORE

(I'll go steal some money from my master to make me
handsome.) Pray pardon me, I must go see a ship discharged.

BELLAMIRA

Canst thou be so unkind to leave me thus?

PILIA-BORZA

And ye did but know how she loves you, sir. 55

ITHAMORE

Nay, I care not how much she loves me; sweet Allamira, would I had my master's wealth for thy sake.

PILIA-BORZA

And you can have it, sir, and if you please.

ITHAMORE

If 'twere above ground I could, and would have it; but
he hides and buries it up as partridges do their eggs, 60
under the earth.

PILIA-BORZA

And is't not possible to find it out?

ITHAMORE

By no means possible.

BELLAMIRA

(What shall we do with this base villain then?

PILIA-BORZA

Let me alone, do but you speak him fair.) 65
But you know some secrets of the Jew, which if they were
revealed, would do him harm.

ITHAMORE

Ay, and such as – Go to, no more, I'll make him send
me half he has, and glad he scapes so too. Pen and ink:
I'll write unto him, we'll have money straight. 70

51–3 ed. (Q I'le ... to / Make ... hansome: / Pray ... discharg'd.)
52 *discharged* unloaded
55 *And* If
56–7 ed. (Q Nay ... me; / Sweet ... sake.)
56–7 *Allamira* Although Q frequently employs variant forms of characters' names,
    this variation suggests misspeaking.
58 *and if* if
59–61 ed. (Q If ... it; / But ... doe / Their ... earth.)
65 ed. (Q Let ... fair:)
    let me alone leave it to me
    speak him fair talk sweetly to him
68–70 ed. (Q I ... more / I'le ... too. / Pen and Inke: / I'le ... strait.)
68 *Go to* (exclamation) go on; come, come
69 *scapes* escapes
70 *straight* right away

PILIA-BORZA

Send for a hundred crowns at least.

ITHAMORE

Ten hundred thousand crowns, – (*He writes*) 'Master Barabas'.

PILIA-BORZA

Write not so submissively, but threatening him.

ITHAMORE

'Sirrah Barabas, send me a hundred crowns.'   75

PILIA-BORZA

Put in two hundred at least.

ITHAMORE

'I charge thee send me three hundred by this bearer, and this shall be your warrant; if you do not, no more but so.'

PILIA-BORZA

Tell him you will confess.   80

ITHAMORE

'Otherwise I'll confess all.' Vanish and return in a twinkle.

PILIA-BORZA

Let me alone, I'll use him in his kind.   [*Exit*]

ITHAMORE

Hang him Jew.

BELLAMIRA

Now, gentle Ithamore, lie in my lap.   85
Where are my maids? Provide a running banquet;
Send to the merchant, bid him bring me silks,
Shall Ithamore my love go in such rags?

ITHAMORE

And bid the jeweller come hither too.

72–3 ed. (Q *one line*)

72 *He writes* (marginally after line 71 in Q)

75 *Sirrah* a disrespectful form of address (see I.i.70)

77–9 ed. (Q I . . . this / Shall . . . so.)

78 *no more but so* As Craik points out, this vague threat – something like 'you know what I mean' – is given a more precise form by Pilia-Borza's subsequent suggestions.

81 *all.' Vanish* ed. (Q all, vanish)

81–2 *in a twinkle* instantly

83 *use* treat

in his kind according to his nature. Bawcutt (citing Tilley, J 52) observes that to 'use someone like a Jew' later became proverbial for ill-treatment.

85 *lie in my lap* used with sexual implication

86 *running banquet* hastily prepared banquet

BELLAMIRA

I have no husband, sweet, I'll marry thee.   90

ITHAMORE

Content, but we will leave this paltry land,
And sail from hence to Greece, to lovely Greece,
I'll be thy Jason, thou my golden fleece;
Where painted carpets o'er the meads are hurled,
And Bacchus' vineyards o'er-spread the world: 95
Where woods and forests go in goodly green,
I'll be Adonis, thou shalt be Love's Queen.
The meads, the orchards, and the primrose lanes,
Instead of sedge and reed, bear sugar canes:
Thou in those groves, by Dis above,   100
Shalt live with me and be my love.

BELLAMIRA

Whither will I not go with gentle Ithamore?

Enter PILIA-BORZA

ITHAMORE

How now? Hast thou the gold?

PILIA-BORZA

Yes.

ITHAMORE

But came it freely, did the cow give down her milk freely?   105

PILIA-BORZA

At reading of the letter, he stared and stamped and
turned aside, I took him by the beard, and looked upon
him thus; told him he were best to send it, then he
hugged and embraced me.

91 *Content* agreed
93 *Jason ... fleece* According to the Greek myth, Jason and the Argonauts recovered
   the magical golden fleece from Colchis.
94 *painted carpets* used metaphorically for bright flowers
   meads meadows
95 *Bacchus* Roman name for Dionysus, god of wine
96 *go* are dressed in
97 *Adonis ... Love's Queen* In classical myth and verse, Adonis was a beautiful youth
   beloved by Venus, goddess of love.
99 *sedge* coarse grass
100 *Dis* Roman god (Greek Hades, Pluto) of the underworld; i.e. by no means 'above'
101 This alludes (probably parodically) to Marlowe's own lyric 'The Passionate
    Shepherd to his Love', which begins 'Come live with me and be my love'.
105 *give down her milk* let flow her milk
106–9 ed. (Q At ... turnd / Aside ... thus; / Told ... me.)
106 *stared* ed. (Q sterd)
107 *took him by the beard* a serious insult
    thus an indication of staged action (see I.ii.347)

ITHAMORE
  Rather for fear than love.   110
PILIA-BORZA
  Then like a Jew he laughed and jeered, and told me he
  loved me for your sake, and said what a faithful servant
  you had been.
ITHAMORE
  The more villain he to keep me thus: here's goodly 'parel,
  is there not?   115
PILIA-BORZA
  To conclude, he gave me ten crowns.
ITHAMORE
  But ten? I'll not leave him worth a grey groat, give me a
  ream of paper, we'll have a kingdom of gold for't.
PILIA-BORZA
  Write for five hundred crowns.
ITHAMORE
  [*Writes*] 'Sirrah Jew, as you love your life send me five   120
  hundred crowns, and give the bearer one hundred.' Tell
  him I must have't.
PILIA-BORZA
  I warrant your worship shall have't.
ITHAMORE
  And if he ask why I demand so much, tell him,
  I scorn to write a line under a hundred crowns.   125
PILIA-BORZA
  You'd make a rich poet, sir. I am gone.   *Exit*
ITHAMORE
  Take thou the money, spend it for my sake.
BELLAMIRA
  'Tis not thy money, but thy self I weigh:
  Thus Bellamira esteems of gold;   [*Throws it aside*]
  But thus of thee.   *Kiss*[*es*] *him* 130

112–13 ed. (Q *one line*)
114–15 ed. (Q The ... thus: / Here's ... not?)
    'parel clothing
116 *ten crowns* as a tip
117–18 ed. (Q But ... giue / Me ... for't.)
117 *grey groat* i.e. an insignificant amount
118 *ream* with an apparent pun on 'realm'
120–2 ed. (Q Sirra ... crowns, / And ... hau't.)
121 *one hundred* ed. (Q 100)
128 *weigh* value

ITHAMORE

    That kiss again; she runs division of my lips.

    What an eye she casts on me! It twinkles like a star.

BELLAMIRA

    Come my dear love, let's in and sleep together.

ITHAMORE

    Oh that ten thousand nights were put in one,

    that we might sleep seven years together afore we wake.   135

BELLAMIRA

    Come amorous wag, first banquet and then sleep.

                                       [Exeunt]

[Act IV, Scene iii]

Enter BARABAS *reading a letter*

BARABAS

    'Barabas send me three hundred crowns.'

    Plain Barabas: Oh that wicked courtesan!

    He was not wont to call me Barabas.

    'Or else I will confess': ay, there it goes:

    But if I get him *coupe de gorge*, for that.   5

    He sent a shaggy tottered staring slave,

    That when he speaks, draws out his grisly beard,

    And winds it twice or thrice about his ear;

    Whose face has been a grindstone for men's swords,

    His hands are hacked, some fingers cut quite off;   10

    Who when he speaks, grunts like a hog, and looks

    Like one that is employed in catzerie,

    And crossbiting, such a rogue

---

131 *runs division of* plays musically upon

132 *me!* ed. (Q What ... me? / It ... Starre.)

134–5 Craik accurately sums up this speech as 'Marlowesque verse, tailing off into bathetic prose'.

135 ed. (Q That ... afore / We wake.)

136 *wag* a term of endearment, impudent youth

  3 *wont* accustomed

  4 *there it goes* i.e. this shows his intentions

  5 *coupe de gorge* (French) [I'll] cut [his] throat

    that. ed. (Q that)

  6 *tottered* tattered

 12 *in catzerie* i.e. in pimping; from Italian 'cazzo' (cf. IV.i.20)

 13 *crossbiting,* ed. (Q crossbiting)

    crossbiting cheating (probably implying reciprocity, as in wronging a wrongdoer)

As is the husband to a hundred whores:
And I by him must send three hundred crowns.   15
Well, my hope is, he will not stay there still;
And when he comes: Oh that he were but here!

Enter PILIA-BORZA

PILIA-BORZA
Jew, I must ha' more gold.
BARABAS
Why want'st thou any of thy tale?
PILIA-BORZA
No; but three hundred will not serve his turn.   20
BARABAS
Not serve his turn, sir?
PILIA-BORZA
No sir; and therefore I must have five hundred more.
BARABAS
I'll rather –
PILIA-BORZA
Oh good words, sir, and send it you were best; see, there's
his letter.   25
BARABAS
Might he not as well come as send? Pray bid him come
and fetch it; what he writes for you, ye shall have straight.
PILIA-BORZA
Ay, and the rest too, or else –
BARABAS
(I must make this villain away.) Please you dine with me,
sir, and you shall be most heartily (poisoned).   30
PILIA-BORZA
No god-a-mercy, shall I have these crowns?

14 *husband ... whores* i.e. either a pimp who 'husbands' the resources of a hundred
   prostitutes, or a swindler who claims to be the husband of prostitutes in order to
   blackmail their clients
16 *still* forever
19 *want'st ... tale?* are you missing any of your desired amount?
20 *serve his turn* be sufficient for his purposes
24–5 ed. (Q Oh ... see, / There's ... letter.)
24 *good words* do not speak so aggressively (cf. V.ii.61)
26–7 ed. (Q Might ... him / Come ... streight.)
   what ... for you the bearer's hundred crowns (cf. IV.ii.121)
29 ed. (Q away: please)
29–30 ed. (Q I ... dine / With ... poyson'd.) Q's marginal '*aside*' does not indicate
   how much of this speech is aside; cf. Barabas's unexpected final words (e.g.
   II.iii.68).

BARABAS

I cannot do it, I have lost my keys.

PILIA-BORZA

Oh, if that be all, I can pick ope your locks.

BARABAS

Or climb up to my counting-house window: you know
my meaning. 35

PILIA-BORZA

I know enough, and therefore talk not to me of your
counting-house; the gold, or know Jew it is in my power
to hang thee.

BARABAS

(I am betrayed.)
'Tis not five hundred crowns that I esteem, 40
I am not moved at that: this angers me,
That he who knows I love him as myself
Should write in this imperious vein! Why sir,
You know I have no child, and unto whom
Should I leave all but unto Ithamore? 45

PILIA-BORZA

Here's many words but no crowns; the crowns.

BARABAS

Commend me to him, sir, most humbly,
And unto your good mistress as unknown.

PILIA-BORZA

Speak, shall I have 'em, sir?

BARABAS

Sir here they are. [*Gives gold*] 50
(Oh that I should part with so much gold!)
Here take 'em, fellow, with as good a will –
(As I would see thee hanged.) Oh, love stops my breath:
Never loved man servant as I do Ithamore.

PILIA-BORZA

I know it, sir. 55

BARABAS

Pray when, sir, shall I see you at my house?

34–5 ed. (Q Or ... window: / You ... meaning.) Barabas implies knowledge of the
burglary attempt in III.i.

37–8 ed. (Q *one line*)

Counting-house; ed. (Q Counting-house,)

43 *vein!* ed. (Q vaine?)

48 *as unknown* a polite locution: unknown to Barabas

53 ed. (Q – *As I wud see thee hang'd*; oh, loue stops my breath:)

PILIA-BORZA
  Soon enough to your cost, sir: fare you well.   *Exit*
BARABAS
  Nay to thine own cost, villain, if thou com'st.
  Was ever Jew tormented as I am?
  To have a shag-rag knave to come –   60
  Three hundred crowns, and then five hundred crowns?
  Well, I must seek a means to rid 'em all,
  And presently: for in his villainy
  He will tell all he knows and I shall die for't.
  I have it.   65
  I will in some disguise go see the slave,
  And how the villain revels with my gold.   *Exit*

[Act IV, Scene iv]

Enter COURTESAN [BELLAMIRA], ITHAMORE, PILIA-BORZA

BELLAMIRA
  I'll pledge thee, love, and therefore drink it off.
ITHAMORE
  Say'st thou me so? Have at it; and do you hear?
                                    [*Whispers to her*]
BELLAMIRA
  Go to, it shall be so.
ITHAMORE
  Of that condition, I will drink it up; here's to thee.
BELLAMIRA
  Nay, I'll have all or none.   5
ITHAMORE
  There, if thou lov'st me do not leave a drop.
BELLAMIRA
  Love thee, fill me three glasses.

---

  57 ed. (Q Soone ... Sir: / Fare ... well.)
  60 *shag rag* ragged
       come – ed. (Q come) Many editors conjecture a missing word such as 'demand'
       or 'convey' after 'come'.
  63 *presently* immediately
  64–5 ed. (Q *one line*)
   2 *me* to me
   4 *Of* On
   5 *Bellamira* ed. (Q Pil.) As Bawcutt argues, attribution of this line to Bellamira
       makes sense, both because she is engaged in a ritual of drinking toasts with
       Ithamore and because she has reasons to encourage him to get drunk.

ITHAMORE

Three and fifty dozen, I'll pledge thee.

PILIA-BORZA

Knavely spoke, and like a knight at arms.

ITHAMORE

Hey *Rivo Castiliano*, a man's a man.   10

BELLAMIRA

Now to the Jew.

ITHAMORE

Ha to the Jew, and send me money you were best.

PILIA-BORZA

What would'st thou do if he should send thee none?

ITHAMORE

Do nothing; but I know what I know, he's a murderer.

BELLAMIRA

I had not thought he had been so brave a man.   15

ITHAMORE

You knew Mathias and the Governor's son, he and I
killed 'em both, and yet never touched 'em.

PILIA-BORZA

Oh bravely done.

ITHAMORE

I carried the broth that poisoned the nuns, and he and
I, snickle hand too fast, strangled a friar.   20

---

8 *thee.* ed. (Q thee,)

9 *Knavely spoke.* Craik's argument that this phrase plays on 'bravely spoke' (as in
'bravely done' in line 18) with a clever antithesis between 'knave' and 'knight' is
attractive, since this figure would compactly render Pilia-Borza's contempt for
Ithamore and his drunken version of romantic exuberance.

10 *Rivo Castiliano* 'Rivo' is perhaps derived from Spanish *arriba* (up, upwards) and
appears by itself as a drinker's cry (cf. *1 Henry IV* II.iv.108–9). 'Rivo Castiliano'
could also be Italian for 'River of Castile', and thus might suggest a wish for
Spanish wine.

   a man's a man a proverbial assertion of human equality despite social distinction
(cf. Tilley, M 243 and Iago's drinking song with 'A soldier's a man' in *Othello*
II.iii.66)

12 *Ha to the Jew* Craik argues that Ithamore responds to the offer of an ironic toast
to Barabas in the previous line; but it appears more likely that Bellamira proposes
Ithamore turn his attention to extorting money from Barabas and that he here
begins dictating his letter to that effect.

   you i.e. Barabas

14 ed. (Q Doe … know, / He's a murderer.)

16–17 ed. (Q You … and / I … 'em.)

19–20 ed. (Q I … he / And … Fryar.)

20 *I, snickle hand too fast,* ed. (Q I snickle hand too fast,) Unclear; 'snickle' may mean
'snare', so the phrase could mean 'I, with my snaring hand too fast to be escaped'.
'Hand to fist' – a stock phrase for hand to hand combat – has been suggested;

BELLAMIRA

You two alone.

ITHAMORE

We two, and 'twas never known, nor never shall be for me.

PILIA-BORZA

(This shall with me unto the Governor.

BELLAMIRA

And fit it should: but first let's ha' more gold!)
Come gentle Ithamore, lie in my lap.   25

ITHAMORE

Love me little, love me long, let music rumble,
Whilst I in thy incony lap do tumble.

Enter BARABAS *with a lute, disguised*

BELLAMIRA

A French musician, come let's hear your skill?

BARABAS

Must tuna my lute for sound, twang twang first.

ITHAMORE

Wilt drink Frenchman, here's to thee with a – Pox on   30
this drunken hiccup.

BARABAS

Gramercy monsieur.

BELLAMIRA

Prithee, Pilia-Borza, bid the fiddler give me the posy in
his hat there.

PILIA-BORZA

Sirrah, you must give my mistress your posy.   35

BARABAS

A vôtre commandement madame.

---

while Craik follows Kittredge in punctuating as reiterated dialogue 'snicle! hand
to! fast!'

22 ed. (Q We . . . shall / Be for me.)
    for me so far as I am concerned

25 *lie* suggesting sexual intercourse

26 *Love me little, love me long* proverbial (Tilley, L 559)

27 *incony* ed. (Q incoomy) attractive, with an obscene pun, as Craik notes, on
    'coney' as used in Marlowe's translation of Ovid's *Elegies* (I.x): 'The whore stands
    to be bought for each man's money, / And seeks vile wealth by selling of her
    coney'

30 ed. (Q Wilt . . . a – / Pox . . . hick-vp.)
    Pox an oath; literally, venereal disease

32 *Gramercy* thank you

33–4 ed. (Q Prethe . . . me / The . . . there.)
    posy bouquet

36 *A vôtre commandement* (French) At your command

BELLAMIRA
How sweet, my Ithamore, the flowers smell.
ITHAMORE
Like thy breath, sweetheart, no violet like 'em.
PILIA-BORZA
Foh, methinks they stink like a hollyhock.
BARABAS
(So, now I am revenged upon 'em all.   40
The scent thereof was death, I poisoned it.)
ITHAMORE
Play, fiddler, or I'll cut your cats' guts into chitterlings.
BARABAS
Pardonnez-moi, be no in tune yet; so now, now all be in.
ITHAMORE
Give him a crown, and fill me out more wine.
PILIA-BORZA
There's two crowns for thee, play.   45
BARABAS
(How liberally the villain gives me mine own gold.)
PILIA-BORZA
Methinks he fingers very well.
BARABAS
(So did you when you stole my gold.)
PILIA-BORZA
How swift he runs.
BARABAS
(You run swifter when you threw my gold out of my   50
window.)
BELLAMIRA
Musician, hast been in Malta long?
BARABAS
Two, three, four month madame.
ITHAMORE
Dost not know a Jew, one Barabas?
BARABAS
Very mush, monsieur, you no be his man.   55

42 *cats' guts . . . chitterlings* lute strings . . . pork sausages
43 *Pardonnez-moi* ed. (Q Pardona moy) (French) Pardon me. It is not clear whether
   Barabas's French is intended to be as corrupt as his accented English in this
   scene.
44 *fill me out* pour for me
46 Q has a marginal '*aside*' here and at lines 48, 51, 61, 63 and 66.
47 *fingers* plays (with a pun on 'pilfering' that is picked up in Barabas's next line)
49 *runs* executes a rapid sequence of notes
50–1 ed. (Q You . . . of / My Window.)
55 *man* servant (this line is often made a question)

PILIA-BORZA
His man?
ITHAMORE
I scorn the peasant, tell him so.
BARABAS
(He knows it already.)
ITHAMORE
'Tis a strange thing of that Jew, he lives upon pickled
grasshoppers, and sauced mushrumbs.   60
BARABAS
(What a slave's this? The Governor feeds not as I do.)
ITHAMORE
He never put on clean shirt since he was circumcised.
BARABAS
(Oh rascal! I change myself twice a day.)
ITHAMORE
The hat he wears, Judas left under the elder when he
hanged himself.   65
BARABAS
('Twas sent me for a present from the great Cham.)
PILIA-BORZA
A masty slave he is; whither now, fiddler?
BARABAS
Pardonnez moi, monsieur, we be no well.   *Exit*
PILIA-BORZA
Farewell fiddler: one letter more to the Jew.
BELLAMIRA
Prithee sweet love, one more, and write it sharp.   70

59–60 ed. (Q 'Tis ... vpon / Pickled ... Mushrumbs.)
60 *sauced mushrumbs* seasoned mushrooms
61 ed. (Q What ... this? / The ... doe.)
62 *circumcised.* ed. (Q circumcis'd)
64–5 ed. (Q The ... Elder / When ... himselfe.)
   Judas ... himself See Matthew 27; the elder tree is traditional, but the hat is
   apparently Marlowe's invention.
66 *great Cham* emperor (Khan) of the Mongols, Tartars and Chinese
67 ed. (Q A ... is; / Whether ... Fidler?)
   masty fattened, as a swine; or big-bodied. Craik amends to 'nasty', and Bawcutt
   suggests 'musty', but the metaphor of swinishness and the repulsive sense of
   physicality are appropriate to the prejudices of the speakers.
   whither ed. (Q whether)
70 *sharp* sharply worded

ITHAMORE

No, I'll send by word of mouth now; bid him deliver thee
a thousand crowns, by the same token, that the nuns
loved rice, that Friar Bernardine slept in his own clothes,
any of 'em will do it.

PILIA-BORZA

Let me alone to urge it now I know the meaning.   75

ITHAMORE

The meaning has a meaning; come let's in:
To undo a Jew is charity, and not sin.

Exeunt

Act V [Scene i]

Enter GOVERNOR [FERNEZE], KNIGHTS, MARTIN DEL BOSCO [*and*
OFFICERS]

FERNEZE

Now, gentlemen, betake you to your arms,
And see that Malta be well fortified;
And it behoves you to be resolute;
For Calymath having hovered here so long,
Will win the town, or die before the walls.   5

KNIGHT

And die he shall, for we will never yield.

Enter COURTESAN [BELLAMIRA] *and* PILIA-BORZA

BELLAMIRA

Oh bring us to the Governor.

FERNEZE

Away with her, she is a courtesan.

BELLAMIRA

Whate'er I am, yet Governor hear me speak;
I bring thee news by whom thy son was slain: 10
Mathias did it not, it was the Jew.

PILIA-BORZA

Who, besides the slaughter of these gentlemen,
Poisoned his own daughter and the nuns,
Strangled a friar, and I know not what

71–4 ed. (Q No . . . now; / Bid . . . same / Token . . . *Bernardine* / Slept . . . clothes, /
   Any . . . it.)

76 *The meaning has a meaning* Unclear; perhaps Ithamore pretends sagacity and
   deep policy – such pretension would maintain his general parallelism with
   Barabas.

 6 *Knight* Many editors designate as 1 Knight.

Mischief beside.
FERNEZE   Had we but proof of this.   15
BELLAMIRA
   Strong proof, my lord, his man's now at my lodging
   That was his agent, he'll confess it all.
FERNEZE
   Go fetch him straight,   [*Exeunt* OFFICERS]
                    I always feared that Jew.

         Enter [OFFICERS *with*] JEW [BARABAS], ITHAMORE

BARABAS
   I'll go alone, dogs do not hale me thus.
ITHAMORE
   Nor me neither, I cannot outrun you constable, oh my   20
   belly.
BARABAS
   (One dram of powder more had made all sure,
      What a damned slave was I!)
FERNEZE
   Make fires, heat irons, let the rack be fetched.
KNIGHT
   Nay stay, my lord, 't may be he will confess.   25
BARABAS
   Confess; what mean you, lords, who should confess?
FERNEZE
   Thou and thy Turk; 'twas you that slew my son.
ITHAMORE
   Guilty, my lord, I confess; your son and Mathias
   Were both contracted unto Abigail,
   Forged a counterfeit challenge.   30
BARABAS
   Who carried that challenge?
ITHAMORE
   I carried it, I confess, but who writ it? Marry even he
   that strangled Bernardine, poisoned the nuns, and his
   own daughter.

   16–17 ed. (Q Strong . . . my / Lodging . . . all.)
   18 *straight* immediately
   19 *hale* drag
   20 To 'outrun the constable' is proverbial (Tilley, C 615).
   23 *damned slave* fool
       I! ed. (Q I?)
   30 Many editors insert an initial 'he', although in the light of questions about agency
       in this scene, it may be worthwhile to keep the ambiguity of Ithamore's phrasing.
   32–4 ed. (Q I . . . it? / Marry . . . the / Nuns . . . daughter.)
       marry interjection, 'why, to be sure'

FERNEZE

Away with him, his sight is death to me.   35

BARABAS

For what? You men of Malta, hear me speak;

She is a courtesan and he a thief,

And he my bondman, let me have law,

For none of this can prejudice my life.

FERNEZE

Once more away with him; you shall have law.   40

BARABAS

Devils do your worst, I live in spite of you.

As these have spoke so be it to their souls.

(I hope the poisoned flowers will work anon.)

　　　　　　　　[*Exeunt* OFFICERS *with* BARABAS, ITHAMORE,
　　　　　　　　　　　　BELLAMIRA, *and* PILIA-BORZA]

　　　　　　Enter [MATHIAS'S] MOTHER [KATHERINE]

KATHERINE

Was my Mathias murdered by the Jew?

Ferneze, 'twas thy son that murdered him.   45

FERNEZE

Be patient, gentle madam, it was he,

He forged the daring challenge made them fight.

KATHERINE

Where is the Jew, where is that murderer?

FERNEZE

In prison till the law has passed on him.

---

35 Cf. in *The Spanish Tragedy* the Viceroy's irate dismissal of the man he believes to
　　have murdered his son – 'Away with him, his sight is second hell' (I.iii.89).

38 *bondman* slave, serf

38–40 *let me have law . . . you shall have law* Echoes of this phrasing in Shakespeare's
　　Merchant of Venice are pronounced: Shylock's demand 'I crave the law' (IV.i.204)
　　and Portia's ironic acquiescence 'The Jew shall have all justice' (319) accentuate
　　the play's representation of values and communities in confrontation. The charge
　　of legalism has been a traditional feature of Christian responses to Judaism.

39 *life.* ed. (Q life:)

41 *Devils . . . you* These lines are frequently considered to be an aside, and many
　　editors amend Q's 'I live' to 'I'll live', but the defiance in Barabas's voice is
　　elsewhere evident in this scene, and 'I live in spite of you' is a notable instance
　　of that heroic discourse which frequently comes in for ironic treatment in the
　　play (e.g. II.ii.56).

42–3 ed. (Q As . . . soules: / I . . . anon.)

42 *so be it to* so let it be charged against

43 *anon* immediately

49 *passed* passed judgement

Enter OFFICER

OFFICER
  My lord, the courtesan and her man are dead;   50
  So is the Turk, and Barabas the Jew.
FERNEZE
  Dead?
OFFICER
  Dead, my lord, and here they bring his body.

  [*Enter* OFFICERS, *carrying* BARABAS *as dead*]

BOSCO
  This sudden death of his is very strange.
FERNEZE
  Wonder not at it, sir, the heavens are just.   55
  Their deaths were like their lives, then think not of 'em.
  Since they are dead, let them be buried.
  For the Jew's body, throw that o'er the walls,
  To be a prey for vultures and wild beasts.

  [BARABAS *thrown down*]

  So, now away and fortify the town.   60
                    Exeunt [*all except* BARABAS]
BARABAS
  What, all alone? Well fare sleepy drink.
  I'll be revenged on this accursèd town;
  For by my means Calymath shall enter in.
  I'll help to slay their children and their wives,
  To fire the churches, pull their houses down,   65
  Take my goods too, and seize upon my lands:
  I hope to see the Governor a slave,
  And, rowing in a galley, whipped to death.

  Enter CALYMATH, BASHAWS, TURKS

CALYMATH
  Whom have we there, a spy?
BARABAS
  Yes, my good lord, one that can spy a place   70

_____

60 *So* A typical indication of the accomplishment of stage action; presumably Barabas's body is here thrown 'o'er the walls'. Subsequent lines are delivered from
  outside the city walls.
61 *Well fare* blessings on
  sleepy sleep-inducing
64–5 This is a typically Marlovian invocation of destruction (see *Edward II* I.iv.100–
  2; *Massacre at Paris* V.v.61–4).

Where you may enter, and surprise the town:
My name is Barabas; I am a Jew.

CALYMATH
Art thou that Jew whose goods we heard were sold
For tribute money?

BARABAS   The very same, my lord:
And since that time they have hired a slave my man   75
To accuse me of a thousand villainies:
I was imprisoned, but 'scaped their hands.

CALYMATH
Didst break prison?

BARABAS
No, no:
I drank of poppy and cold mandrake juice;   80
And being asleep, belike they thought me dead,
And threw me o'er the walls: so, or how else,
The Jew is here, and rests at your command.

CALYMATH
'Twas bravely done: but tell me, Barabas,
Canst thou, as thou reportest, make Malta ours?   85

BARABAS
Fear not, my lord, for here against the sluice,
The rock is hollow, and of purpose digged,
To make a passage for the running streams
And common channels of the city.
Now whilst you give assault unto the walls,   90
I'll lead five hundred soldiers through the vault,
And rise with them i' th' middle of the town,
Open the gates for you to enter in,
And by this means the city is your own.

CALYMATH
If this be true, I'll make thee Governor.   95

BARABAS
And if it be not true, then let me die.

CALYMATH
Thou'st doomed thyself, assault it presently.

                                              Exeunt

---

80 *poppy ... mandrake* sleep-inducing potions
81 *belike* probably
86 *sluice* ed. (Q truce)
89 *common channels* public sewers
97 *doomed* sentenced
   presently at once

[Act V, Scene ii]

Alarms. Enter TURKS, BARABAS, [*with*] GOVERNOR [FERNEZE]
and KNIGHTS *prisoners*

CALYMATH
Now vail your pride you captive Christians,
And kneel for mercy to your conquering foe:
Now where's the hope you had of haughty Spain?
Ferneze, speak, had it not been much better
To keep thy promise than be thus surprised?   5
FERNEZE
What should I say, we are captives and must yield.
CALYMATH
Ay, villains, you must yield, and under Turkish yokes
Shall groaning bear the burden of our ire;
And Barabas, as erst we promised thee,
For thy desert we make thee Governor;   10
Use them at thy discretion.
BARABAS   Thanks, my lord.
FERNEZE
Oh fatal day to fall into the hands
Of such a traitor and unhallowed Jew!
What greater misery could heaven inflict?
CALYMATH
'Tis our command: and Barabas, we give   15
To guard thy person, these our Janizaries:
Entreat them well, as we have usèd thee.
And now, brave Bashaws, come, we'll walk about
The ruined town, and see the wrack we made:
Farewell brave Jew, farewell great Barabas.   20
                    Exeunt [CALYMATH *and* BASHAWS]
BARABAS
May all good fortune follow Calymath.
And now, as entrance to our safety,
To prison with the Governor and these
Captains, his consorts and confederates.

1 *vail* abase (see II.ii.11)
5 *To keep* ed. (Q To kept)
9 *erst* formerly
10 *thee Governor;* ed. (Q the Governor,)
16 *Janizaries* Turkish infantry. On the dangers of relying upon Janizaries, see Machiavelli, *The Prince* XVIII.
17 *Entreat* treat
19 *wrack* destruction
22 *entrance to our safety* first step in our security

FERNEZE
 Oh villain, heaven will be revenged on thee.   25
    Exeunt [TURKS *with* FERNEZE *and* KNIGHTS]
BARABAS
 Away, no more, let him not trouble me.
 Thus hast thou gotten, by thy policy,
 No simple place, no small authority,
 I now am Governor of Malta; true,
 But Malta hates me, and in hating me   30
 My life's in danger, and what boots it thee
 Poor Barabas, to be the Governor,
 Whenas thy life shall be at their command?
 No, Barabas, this must be looked into;
 And since by wrong thou got'st authority,   35
 Maintain it bravely by firm policy,
 At least unprofitably lose it not:
 For he that liveth in authority,
 And neither gets him friends, nor fills his bags,
 Lives like the ass that Aesop speaketh of,   40
 That labours with a load of bread and wine,
 And leaves it off to snap on thistle tops:
 But Barabas will be more circumspect.
 Begin betimes, Occasion's bald behind,
 Slip not thine opportunity, for fear too late   45
 Thou seek'st for much, but canst not compass it.
 Within here.

   Enter GOVERNOR [FERNEZE] *with a* GUARD

FERNEZE
 My lord?

31 *boots* avails
33 *Whenas* seeing that
39 *bags* purse
40–2 The fable may not be from Aesop, but the proverbial point is clear enough:
  the donkey does not profit from his labours but eats common thistles (cf. *Julius*
  Caesar IV.i.21–8).
44 *betimes* quickly
  Occasion's bald behind As traditionally depicted, Occasion or Opportunity is a
  figure who must be grabbed by her long forelock before she passes because the
  rest of her head is bald.
45 *slip not* do not let slip away
46 *compass* achieve
  it. ed. (Q it)

BARABAS

Ay, 'lord', thus slaves will learn.
Now Governor stand by there – wait within –   50
                       [*Exit* GUARD]
This is the reason that I sent for thee;
Thou seest thy life, and Malta's happiness,
Are at my arbitrament; and Barabas
At his discretion may dispose of both:
Now tell me, Governor, and plainly too,   55
What think'st thou shall become of it and thee?

FERNEZE

This; Barabas, since things are in thy power,
I see no reason but of Malta's wrack,
Nor hope of thee but extreme cruelty,
Nor fear I death, nor will I flatter thee.   60

BARABAS

Governor, good words, be not so furious;
'Tis not thy life which can avail me aught,
Yet you do live, and live for me you shall:
And as for Malta's ruin, think you not
'Twere slender policy for Barabas   65
To dispossess himself of such a place?
For sith, as once you said, within this isle
In Malta here, that I have got my goods,
And in this city still have had success,
And now at length am grown your Governor,   70
Yourselves shall see it shall not be forgot:
For as a friend not known, but in distress,
I'll rear up Malta now remediless.

FERNEZE

Will Barabas recover Malta's loss?
Will Barabas be good to Christians?   75

BARABAS

What wilt thou give me, Governor, to procure
A dissolution of the slavish bands

50 *there – wait within –* ed. (Q there, wait within,) Barabas appears to want Ferneze to stay and the guard to depart.
53 *arbitrament* disposal
58 *no reason but of* no alternative but
61 *good words* i.e. bravely spoken
63 *Yet* still
   for me as far as I am concerned
67 *sith* since
69 *still* continually
72 *as a friend not known, but in distress* as a friend who is unrecognized until the moment of need

Wherein the Turk hath yoked your land and you?
What will you give me if I render you
The life of Calymath, surprise his men,　　　　　　　　80
And in an out-house of the city shut
His soldiers, till I have consumed 'em all with fire?
What will you give him that procureth this?

FERNEZE
Do but bring this to pass which thou pretendest,
Deal truly with us as thou intimatest,　　　　　　　　85
And I will send amongst the citizens
And by my letters privately procure
Great sums of money for thy recompense:
Nay more, do this, and live thou Governor still.

BARABAS
Nay, do thou this, Ferneze, and be free;　　　　　　　90
Governor, I enlarge thee, live with me,
Go walk about the city, see thy friends:
Tush, send not letters to 'em, go thyself,
And let me see what money thou canst make;
Here is my hand that I'll set Malta free:　　　　　　　95
And thus we cast it: to a solemn feast
I will invite young Selim-Calymath,
Where be thou present only to perform
One stratagem that I'll impart to thee,
Wherein no danger shall betide thy life,　　　　　　　100
And I will warrant Malta free for ever.

FERNEZE
Here is my hand, believe me, Barabas,
I will be there, and do as thou desirest;
When is the time?

BARABAS　　　　　　　Governor, presently.
For Calymath, when he hath viewed the town,　　　　　105
Will take his leave and sail toward Ottoman.

FERNEZE
Then will I, Barabas, about this coin,
And bring it with me to thee in the evening.

81 *out-house* outlying building
91 *enlarge* free
96 *cast* plot
100 *betide* happen to
101 *warrant* promise
106 *toward Ottoman.* ed. (Q toward, Ottoman,) i.e. Turkey
107 *about this coin* go about getting this money

BARABAS
   Do so, but fail not; now farewell Ferneze:
                       [*Exit* FERNEZE]
   And thus far roundly goes the business: 110
   Thus loving neither, will I live with both,
   Making a profit of my policy;
   And he from whom my most advantage comes,
   Shall be my friend.
   This is the life we Jews are used to lead;   115
   And reason too, for Christians do the like:
   Well, now about effecting this device:
   First to surprise great Selim's soldiers,
   And then to make provision for the feast,
   That at one instant all things may be done,   120
   My policy detests prevention:
   To what event my secret purpose drives,
   I know; and they shall witness with their lives.   *Exit*

[Act V, Scene iii]

Enter CALYMATH, BASHAWS

CALYMATH
   Thus have we viewed the city, seen the sack,
   And caused the ruins to be new repaired,
   Which with our bombards' shot and basilisks',
   We rent in sunder at our entry:
   And now I see the situation,   5
   And how secure this conquered island stands
   Environed with the Mediterranean Sea,
   Strong countermured with other petty isles;

110 *roundly* fairly, successfully
115 *used to* accustomed to
116 *And reason too* And with good reason
121 *prevention* being forestalled
122–3 The phrasing recalls that of Hieronimo's antagonist, Lorenzo, in *The Spanish Tragedy* III.iv.82–8.
  1 *sack* plundering
  3 *bombards* cannons of an early type, throwing large shot or stone
    basilisks' ed. (Q Basiliske) brass cannon
 4–12 The order here printed preserves that of Q; the lineation of this speech has been much debated, with some editors arguing line 10 is misplaced and belongs between lines 4 and 5, with a substitution of 'where' for 'when' in line 11.
  8 *countermured* ed. (Q contermin'd) defended

And toward Calabria backed by Sicily,
Two lofty turrets that command the town.   10
When Syracusian Dionysius reigned;
I wonder how it could be conquered thus?

Enter a MESSENGER

MESSENGER
From Barabas, Malta's Governor, I bring
A message unto mighty Calymath;
Hearing his sovereign was bound for sea,   15
To sail to Turkey, to great Ottoman,
He humbly would entreat your majesty
To come and see his homely citadel,
And banquet with him ere thou leav'st the isle.
CALYMATH
To banquet with him in his citadel;   20
I fear me, messenger, to feast my train
Within a town of war so lately pillaged,
Will be too costly and too troublesome:
Yet would I gladly visit Barabas.
For well has Barabas deserved of us.   25
MESSENGER
Selim, for that, thus saith the Governor,
That he hath in store a pearl so big,
So precious, and withal so orient,
As be it valued but indifferently,
The price thereof will serve to entertain   30
Selim and all his soldiers for a month;

---

9 *toward Calabria backed by Sicily* in the direction of Calabria (in Italy) defended
  by Sicily
10 *lofty turrets* perhaps the forts of Saint Angelo and Saint Elmo
11 *Syracusian Dionysius* probably Dionysius I (c. 430–367 B.C.), tyrant of Syracuse
  and aggressive military leader; from Plato to the end of the sixteenth century, a
  figure standing for oppressive tyranny
11–12 'When' Dionysius reigned, Calymath reasons, the military-political advan-
  tages of imperial tyranny would have compounded Malta's natural impregnability,
  so could it really have been conquered this easily? The question mark may
  indicate a tone mixing wonder with something like a rhetorical question.
16 *great Ottoman* the sultan of Turkey
20 *citadel;* ed. (Q Citadell,)
21 *train* retinue
22 *of* by
   lately recently
26 *for that* concerning that objection
27 *in store* in reserve
28 *so orient* so lustrous

Therefore he humbly would entreat your highness
Not to depart till he has feasted you.

CALYMATH

I cannot feast my men in Malta walls,
Except he place his tables in the streets.   35

MESSENGER

Know, Selim, that there is a monastery
Which standeth as an out-house to the town;
There will he banquet them, but thee at home,
With all thy Bashaws and brave followers.

CALYMATH

Well, tell the Governor we grant his suit,   40
We'll in this summer evening feast with him.

MESSENGER

I shall, my lord.   *Exit*

CALYMATH

And now bold Bashaws, let us to our tents,
And meditate how we may grace us best
To solemnize our Governor's great feast.   45

                                               Exeunt

[Act V, Scene iv]

Enter GOVERNOR [FERNEZE], KNIGHTS, [MARTIN] DEL BOSCO

FERNEZE

In this, my countrymen, be ruled by me,
Have special care that no man sally forth
Till you shall hear a culverin discharged
By him that bears the linstock, kindled thus;
Then issue out and come to rescue me,   5
For happily I shall be in distress,
Or you releasèd of this servitude.

1 KNIGHT

Rather than thus to live as Turkish thralls,
What will we not adventure?

FERNEZE

On then, begone.

---

35 *Except* unless
44 *meditate how we may grace* consider how we may equip
 3 *culverin* an elongated cannon
 4 *linstock* a staff holding the flame for igniting the charge
 6 *happily* perchance
 8 *thralls* slaves
 9 *adventure* risk

KNIGHTS   Farewell grave Governor.   10

                                         [*Exeunt*]

[Act V, Scene v]

Enter [BARABAS] *with a hammer above, very busy*; [*and*
CARPENTERS]

BARABAS

How stand the cords? How hang these hinges, fast?
Are all the cranes and pulleys sure?
CARPENTER   All fast.

BARABAS

Leave nothing loose, all levelled to my mind.
Why now I see that you have art indeed.
There, carpenters, divide that gold amongst you: 5
Go swill in bowls of sack and muscadine:
Down to the cellar, taste of all my wines.
CARPENTERS

We shall, my lord, and thank you.

                              Exeunt [CARPENTERS]

BARABAS

And if you like them, drink your fill and die:
For so I live, perish may all the world.   10
Now Selim-Calymath return me word
That thou wilt come, and I am satisfied.

                     Enter MESSENGER

Now sirrah, what, will he come?
MESSENGER

He will; and has commanded all his men
To come ashore, and march through Malta streets,   15
That thou mayst feast them in thy citadel.
BARABAS

Then now are all things as my wish would have 'em,
There wanteth nothing but the Governor's pelf,

10 KNIGHTS ed. (Q *Kni:*)
 2 *Carpenter* ed. (Q *Serv.*)
 3 *levelled to my mind* in keeping with my plan
 6 *sack and muscadine* wines (Spanish and muscatel)
 9 *die* Barabas has poisoned the wine.
10 *so* provided that
12 s.d. located after line 13 in Q
18 *pelf* money, with possible depreciatory sense

Enter GOVERNOR [FERNEZE]

And see he brings it: now, Governor, the sum.
FERNEZE
With free consent a hundred thousand pounds.   20
BARABAS
Pounds say'st thou, Governor? Well since it is no more
I'll satisfy myself with that; nay, keep it still,
For if I keep not promise, trust not me.
And Governor, now partake my policy:
First for his army they are sent before,   25
Entered the monastery, and underneath
In several places are field-pieces pitched,
Bombards, whole barrels full of gunpowder,
That on the sudden shall dissever it,
And batter all the stones about their ears,   30
Whence none can possibly escape alive:
Now as for Calymath and his consorts,
Here have I made a dainty gallery,
The floor whereof, this cable being cut,
Doth fall asunder; so that it doth sink   35
Into a deep pit past recovery.
Here, hold that knife, and when thou seest he comes,
And with his Bashaws shall be blithely set,
A warning-piece shall be shot off from the tower,
To give thee knowledge when to cut the cord,   40
And fire the house; say, will not this be brave?
FERNEZE
Oh excellent! Here, hold thee, Barabas,
I trust thy word, take what I promised thee.
BARABAS
No, Governor, I'll satisfy thee first,
Thou shalt not live in doubt of any thing.   45

18 s.d. located after line 19 in Q
21 *Governor? Well* ed. (Q Gouernor, well)
24 *partake* be acquainted with
27 *field-pieces pitched* light cannon readied
28 *Bombards* large cannon
29 *dissever it* blow up the monastery
33 *dainty* delightful
37 Barabas gives (throws?) the knife to Ferneze.
38 *blithely set* merrily seated at table
39 *warning-piece* signal gun
41 *the house* the monastery
42 *hold thee* Ferneze offers Barabas money.

Stand close, for here they come: [FERNEZE *retires*]
                                why, is not this
A kingly kind of trade to purchase towns
By treachery, and sell 'em by deceit?
Now tell me, worldlings, underneath the sun,
If greater falsehood ever has been done.   50

Enter CALYMATH *and* BASHAWS

CALYMATH
    Come, my companion Bashaws, see I pray
    How busy Barabas is there above
    To entertain us in his gallery;
    Let us salute him. Save thee, Barabas.
BARABAS
    Welcome great Calymath.   55
FERNEZE
    (How the slave jeers at him?)
BARABAS
    Will't please thee, mighty Selim-Calymath,
    To ascend our homely stairs?
CALYMATH
    Ay, Barabas, come Bashaws, attend.
FERNEZE [*Coming forward*]   Stay, Calymath;
    For I will show thee greater courtesy   60
    Than Barabas would have afforded thee.
KNIGHT
    [*Within*] Sound a charge there.

A charge [*sounded*], *the cable cut, a cauldron
discovered* [*into which* BARABAS *falls*]

[*Enter* MARTIN DEL BOSCO *and* KNIGHTS]

CALYMATH
    How now, what means this?

46 *stand close* step aside into concealment
49–50 This boasting address to the audience under the name of 'worldlings' is
    strongly reminiscent of medieval drama.
    sun ed. (Q summe)
54 *salute him. Save* ed. (salute him, Saue)
    save thee God save thee
62 *charge* trumpet signal for attack
    s.d. *discovered* revealed
    Ferneze cuts the rope, opening the trapdoor which Barabas has constructed over
    the cauldron. As Hunter has suggested, the fall into the cauldron strongly recalls
    representations of sinners' punishment in hell. It is appropriate that Barabas
    suffer the punishment for avarice.
63 *this?* ed. (Q this)

BARABAS
  Help, help me, Christians, help.
FERNEZE
  See Calymath, this was devised for thee.   65
CALYMATH
  Treason, treason Bashaws, fly.
FERNEZE
  No, Selim, do not fly;
  See his end first, and fly then if thou canst.
BARABAS
  Oh help me, Selim, help me Christians.
  Governor, why stand you all so pitiless?   70
GOVERNOR
  Should I in pity of thy plaints or thee,
  Accursèd Barabas, base Jew, relent?
  No, thus I'll see thy treachery repaid,
  But wish thou hadst behaved thee otherwise.
BARABAS
  You will not help me then?
FERNEZE   No, villain, no.   75
BARABAS
  And villains, know you cannot help me now.
  Then Barabas breathe forth thy latest fate,
  And in the fury of thy torments, strive
  To end thy life with resolution:
  Know, Governor, 'twas I that slew thy son;   80
  I framed the challenge that did make them meet:
  Know, Calymath, I aimed thy overthrow,
  And had I but escaped this stratagem,
  I would have brought confusion on you all,
  Damned Christians, dogs, and Turkish infidels;   85
  But now begins the extremity of heat
  To pinch me with intolerable pangs:
  Die life, fly soul, tongue curse thy fill and die!   [*Dies*]
CALYMATH
  Tell me, you Christians, what doth this portend?

72 *Accursèd Barabas, base Jew, relent?* ed. (Q Accursed *Barabas*; base Iew relent:)
77 *latest* last
79 *resolution* fortitude
82 *aimed* intended
84 *confusion* destruction
89 *portend* mean

GOVERNOR
   This train he laid to have entrapped thy life;   90
   Now Selim note the unhallowed deeds of Jews:
   Thus he determined to have handled thee,
   But I have rather chose to save thy life.

CALYMATH
   Was this the banquet he prepared for us?
   Let's hence, lest further mischief be pretended.   95

FERNEZE
   Nay, Selim, stay, for since we have thee here,
   We will not let thee part so suddenly:
   Besides, if we should let thee go, all's one,
   For with thy galleys could'st thou not get hence,
   Without fresh men to rig and furnish them.   100

CALYMATH
   Tush, Governor, take thou no care for that,
   My men are all aboard,
   And do attend my coming there by this.

FERNEZE
   Why heard'st thou not the trumpet sound a charge?

CALYMATH
   Yes, what of that?

FERNEZE   Why then the house was fired,   105
   Blown up and all thy soldiers massacred.

CALYMATH
   Oh monstrous treason!

FERNEZE   A Jew's courtesy:
   For he that did by treason work our fall,
   By treason hath delivered thee to us:
   Know therefore, till thy father hath made good   110
   The ruins done to Malta and to us,
   Thou canst not part: for Malta shall be freed,
   Or Selim ne'er return to Ottoman.

CALYMATH
   Nay rather, Christians, let me go to Turkey,
   In person there to meditate your peace;   115
   To keep me here will nought advantage you.

---

  90 *train* plot
  95 *pretended* intended
  98 *all's one* it would not make any difference
103 *attend ... this* anticipate my return at this time
108 *work our fall* achieve our downfall
115 *meditate* plan
116 *nought advantage* do you no good

FERNEZE
> Content thee, Calymath, here thou must stay,
> And live in Malta prisoner; for come call the world
> To rescue thee, so will we guard us now,
> As sooner shall they drink the ocean dry,   120
> Than conquer Malta, or endanger us.
> So march away, and let due praise be given
> Neither to fate nor fortune, but to heaven.

[*Exeunt*]

FINIS

118 *come call the world* were all the world to come
123 *fate ... fortune ... heaven* Ferneze rejects alternative causalities in favour of
    Christian Providence. Whatever other ironies this may carry in the context of the
    play, it is potentially significant that he rejects the notion of fortune's sway, since
    Machiavelli's emphasis on fortune is such a focus in anti-Machiavellian polemic.

APPENDIX

'THE DUTCH CHURCH LIBEL'

Concern about widespread hostility to the 'stranger' community (which numbered about 5,000, or about 4 to 5% of the London populus in the late sixteenth century) and its threat to the peace appears in documentary evidence drawn from every level of Elizabethan government – aldermanic reports, Recorder Fleet-wood's investigations, the Lord Mayor's warnings, records of the Privy Council, Parliamentary proceedings – and the evidence spans the period of composition and production of Marlowe's play.[1] A recently discovered document, which may itself have contributed to the legal difficulties of both Kyd and Marlowe in May 1593, may compactly illustrate the salient terms of popular resentment in the late 1580s and early 1590s.

In May of 1593, the anonymous 'Dutch Church Libel' was appended to one of the foreign Protestant churches in London, warning 'Ye strangers yt doe inhabite in this lande' to 'expect . . . such a fatall day' as that which had disastrously befallen the Huguenot community at the hands of Catholic forces in the 'Paris massacre' of 1572. The charges of this document suggest the atmosphere in which *The Jew of Malta* was written and produced, and they also lend remarkable contemporary impli-cation to Marlowe's play and especially to its representation of Barabas. The abuses attributed to the foreigners by the libel are numerous, but particularly interesting in relation to the play are the following associations: with merchant practices that are called Machiavellian ('Your Machiavellian Marchant spoyles the state') and involve international marketing, deceptive retailing, employ-ing an uprooted underclass as agents and substituting showy 'gawds' for intrinsically valuable 'goods'; with usury ('Your vsery doth leave vs all for deade') and with pursuing more than a single means of livelihood ('every merchant hath three trades at least'); with greedy depredation that is likened to the ritual Jewish cannibalism of anti-Semitic lore ('like the Jewes, you eate us vp as bread') in taking wealth from the impoverished English ('with our store continually you feast'); with religious hypocrisy ('in counterfeitinge religion') and with an insular Jewish zealotry ('in your temples praying'); with displacing the native poor to a mercenary military service on their behalf ('our pore soules, are cleane thrust out of dore / And to the warres are sent abroade . . . / as sacrifice for you'); with both spying for the government ('You are intelligencers to the state & crown') and with desires for

A Libell, fixte vpon the French Church Wall, in London. Anno. 1593.

Ye strangers ye doe inhabit in this lande
Note this same writing doe it vnderstand
Conceit it well for safegard of your lyves
your goods, your children, & your dearest wives
Your Machiavellian Marchant spoyles the state,
your vsery doth leave vs all for deade
Your Artifex, & craftsman works our fate,
And like the Iewes, you eate vs vp as bread
the Marchant doth ingross all kinde of wares
Forestall's the markets, whereso'ere he goes
Sends forth his wares, by Pedlers to the faires,
Retayls at home, & with his horrible showes: Bodesth thowsands
In Baskets your wares trott vp & downe
Caried the streets by the country nation,
you are intelligencers to the state & crowne
And in your harts doe wish an alteracion,
you transport goods, & bring vs gawds good store
Our Leade, our Vittaile, our Ordenance & what nott
That Egipts plagues, vext not the Egyptians more
then you doe vs; then death shall be your lotte
Noe prize comes in but you make claime therto
And Ebvery merchant hath thress trades at least,
And Cutthrote like in selling you vndoe
vs all, & with our store, continually you feast: We cannot suffer long.
Our poore artificers doe starve & dye
For yf they cannot now be set on Worke
And for your Worke more curious to the eye
In Chambers, twenty in one house will lurke,
Raysing of rents, was never knowne before
Liveing farre better then at native home
And our poore soules, are cleane thrust out of dores
And to the warres are sent abroade to rome,
To fight it out for Fraunce & Belgia,
And dy like doggs as sacrifice for you
Expect you therefore such a fatall day
Shortly on you, & yours for to ensewe: as never was seene
Since words nor threates nor any other thinge
canns make you to avoyd this certaine ill
Weele cutt your throtes, in your temples praying
Not paris massacre so much blood did spill
As we will doe iust vengeance on you all
In counterfeitinge religion for your flight
When 'tis well knowne, you are loth, for to be thrall

social 'alteracion', or, alternatively, with representing a financial
internationalism that threatens 'our gracious Queene' by cor-
rupting the English nobility ('With Spanish gold, you all are
infected / And with yt gould our Nobles wink').

The text which follows is that transcribed by Arthur Freeman
from Bodleian Ms. Don. d. 152, and it is reprinted from his
'Marlowe, Kyd, and the Dutch Church Libel' (*ELR* 3 (1973),
44–51) by permission of the editors. Freeman provides an
account of the Libel (the names 'French' and 'Dutch' for the
two churches were often confused) and its relation to anti-
stranger violence as well as to the legal difficulties of Marlowe
and Thomas Kyd in 1593.

A Libell, fixte vpon the French Church Wall, in London. Anno 1593.

Ye strangers yt doe inhabite in this lande
Note this same writing doe it vnderstand
Conceit it well for savegard of your lyves
Your goods, your children, & your dearest wives
Your Machiavellian Marchant spoyles the state,
Your vsery doth leave vs all for deade
Your Artifex, & craftesman works our fate,
And like the Jewes, you eate us vp as bread
The Marchant doth ingross all kinde of wares
Forestall's the markets, whereso 'ere he goe's
Sends forth his wares, by Pedlers to the faires,
Retayle's at home, & with his horrible showes: Vndoeth thowsands
In Baskets your wares trott up & downe
Carried the streets by the country nation,
You are intelligencers to the state & crowne
And in your hartes doe wish an alteracion,
You transport goods, & bring vs gawds good store
Our Leade, our Vittaile, our Ordenance & what nott
That Egipts plagues, vext not the Egyptians more
Then you doe vs; then death shall be your lotte
Noe prize comes in but you make claime therto
And every merchant hath three trades at least,
And Cutthroate like in selling you vndoe
vs all, & with our store continually you feast: We cannot suffer long.
Our pore artificers doe starve & dye
For yt they cannot now be sett on worke
And for your worke more curious to the ey[.]
In Chambers, twenty in one house will lurke,
Raysing of rents, was never knowne before
Living farre better then at native home
And our poore soules, are cleane thrust out of dore

And to the warres are sent abroade to rome,
To fight it out for Fraunce & Belgia,
And dy like dogges as sacrifice for you
Expect you therefore such a fatall day
Shortly on you, & yours for to ensewe: as never was seene.
Since words nor threates not any other thinge
canne make you to avoyd this certaine ill
Weele cutt your throtes, in your temples praying
Not paris massacre so much blood did spill
As we will doe iust vengeance on you all
In counterfeitinge religion for your flight
When 't'is well knowne, you are loth, for to be thrall
your coyne, & you as countryes cause to flight
With Spanish gold, you all are infected
And with yt gould our Nobles wink at feats
Nobles said I? nay men to be reiected,
Upstarts yt enioy the noblest seates
That wound their Countries brest, for lucres sake
And wrong our gracious Queene & Subiects good
By letting strangers make our harts to ake
For which our swords are whet, to shedd their blood
And for a truth let it be vnderstood/   Fly, Flye, & never returne.
per. Tamberlaine

[1] See Archer, *Pursuit of Stability*, pp. 4–5, 132; Pettegree, *Foreign Protestant Communities*, pp. 219f.